Other Books by this Author

Why "U" Do the Things "U" Do
If "U" Can't Praise Him for the Pit,
"U" Can't Make it to the Palace
Please Let the Real "U" Stand Up
Don't Lose Your Head

ARE YOUR
CHILDREN
OUT OF CONTROL?

Dr. Edward A. Patterson

WESTBOW
PRESS
A DIVISION OF THOMAS NELSON

WestBow Press books may be ordered through booksellers or by contacting:

WestBow Press
A Division of Thomas Nelson
1663 Liberty Drive
Bloomington, IN 47403
www.westbowpress.com
1-(866) 928-1240

ISBN: 978-1-4497-9393-7 (sc)

Library of Congress Control Number: 2013908059

Printed in the United States of America.

WestBow Press rev. date: 06/12/2013

Dedication

This book is dedicated to my wife, Brenda, and all of my children and nuclear family, along with my spiritual mother, the late mother Anne Thomas, who ran the race and came in first place.

Table of Contents

Preface

From time to time, many good-hearted people find themselves responding to people in a way that causes them to be ashamed of themselves. They beat themselves up because of the way they responded. They really would like to change that behavior but have no clue as to how to achieve the wanted changes. In my counseling manual, I talk about three kinds of people: the repressed, the suppressed, and the oppressed.

Repressed people are unaware that childhood experiences have an effect on them as adults. These people have blocked the memory due to the intense trauma they experienced. They exhibit periods of depression and have thoughts of suicide. Some may experience inexplicable physical pain. Suppressed people are aware of an incident but, feeling that it has no relevance to them today, suppress the memory. They may exhibit low self-esteem and find it difficult to establish relationships. Oppressed people remember and identify the past trauma but think they have resolved the problem. They may exhibit mood swings, be overly critical of others, and lack victory in their lives.

It is of vital importance for a person to understand what makes them tick. Understanding one's self can lead to the road of recovery. It is my hope that after reading this book, the reader will be motivated to put forth the effort to make any adjustments that are conducive to the newness of life.

CHAPTER

Biological versus Inner Children

The children of today are so much different from children of the baby boomers and previous generations. The children of today start doing things so much earlier than the children of several decades ago. There are so many new distractions for children today. The United States is the leader in child obesity. It wasn't long ago when I was talking to an old buddy. We talked about how things were when we were growing up. We did not spend much time in the house. We played football nearly every day during football season. We played basketball during basketball season. Occasionally, we would get in a little baseball. My buddy reminded me of how we tried to stay out of the house to keep from having to do work inside the house.

We were very active. Kids today have too many inside games. They spend too much time inside playing video games that do not offer any physical conditioning. Along with teaching these young kids to live a sedentary lifestyle, these video games teach kids to live an immoral life. Young ladies are getting pregnant at a much earlier age. Things are not moving at the pace they once did. They move much faster than I would like to see them move. The television today is so much different than it was when I was growing up. I recall when there was not a cuss word said on television. Nowadays a movie is not considered a good movie if it doesn't include cussing. There are movie channels that are influencing young kids to seek an immoral life style. A lot of advertisement on television is sex-oriented.

There are so many phenomena that contribute to the ill behavior of young people today. One of the areas of study I was involved in was early childhood education. I obtained a degree in the field. I got involved with the childcare business with my wife. There is a childcare program that is called More for Four. I knew this would not be a good program for children because it forces four-year-olds to skip one of the stages they need in life. I attended a meeting where the directors of childcare facilities bid on a grant to have the program in their facility. The person heading the meeting made this statement: "We have learned that the children in this program have real problems by the time they reach the third grade because they do not have the foundation necessary to exercise the proper behavior." She then went on to have the people put in their bids for the grant to run the program in their facility. How asinine is that? I couldn't believe I was hearing what I was hearing. What the person was really saying was, "We know we are screwing these children up, but what do we care? There is money to be made."

I believe in cause and effect. I was trying to distinguish the difference between cause and effect, and correlation. It is difficult for me to distinguish the two. In the field of psychology, it is said that there is a correlation between elderly people having a relationship with God along with regular church attendance and being healthier and happier than the those elderly people who do the opposite. Why does psychology not use the phrase *"cause and effect"* here? I think I may be able to answer that question.

Psychology is a field that is independent of any religious affiliation. It is a very lucrative field. If the field of psychology gave credence to religious practices, it may lose its credibility. The money made in this field will come to naught, and the people in the profession will have to find another one. The word *correlation* is an attempt to downplay actual cause and effect. I said all of that to say this; if your children are out of control, there is a reason for it. The next time, I will warn you when I'm going off on a tangent.

Children being out of control come under the guise of cause and effect. In other words, as adults, we have inner children, and these inner children may be out of control. There are many different reasons our inner children may be out of control. There are only a few categories from which to derive these reasons. It is what I call the five painful areas of life.

When parents have inner children that are out of control, it affects the children under their leadership. The five areas of pain are physical abuse, emotional abuse, rejection, molestation, and incest. Many parents have experienced these painful areas. There are those who have experience only one, and there are those who have experienced all of them. There are things we do a certain way because of what we have experienced. This nation is approximately 234 years old. When we look at the experience of the first generation in this country, we see parents who had a concern for their children. Children were taught to be responsible, to be able to carry out responsibilities, and to pass those responsibilities on to the next generation.

I believe it was around the sixties when parents decided that they wanted to live in such a way that allow them to enjoy their lives and to do so would require not having the arduous responsibility of child rearing. It only takes one irresponsible generation to cause an entire nation to go morally bankrupt. The generation I am referring to is the baby-boomer generation. This generation includes people born after the men of the United States came home after World War II. It is also known in spiritual circles as the fig-tree generation. This name references the time in which Israel became a nation, in 1948. The fig-tree generation decided it was time-out for sacrificial living and time for selfish living. The people of this generation did not take into consideration the mess they would be leaving behind.

Each generation is responsible for training the next generation. The baby-buster generation, the generation after the baby boomers, found themselves in a world of hurt because of the previous generation not wanting to grow up and be responsible. Those inner children are out of control and wreaking havoc in the lives of the children in the generation under their leadership. Now we live in a society in which wrong is considered right and right has become obsolete. There is a reason why men are marrying men and women are marrying women. At one time, this was not allowed in the society in which we live.

This is how cause and effect takes place: one generation dropping the ball has put our nation in the grips of judgment, and that generation is the generation in leadership today. We have to pay a price for the wrongs we have done as a nation. God is not a God of condemnation, but He will do what it takes to get His people back on course. I remember during my early years in the military when I was coming up the ranks, a gentleman in my chain of command, when I jokingly told him I was going to disobey a direct order, told me that I would be sorry if I disobeyed his direct order. I said, "What are you going to do, kill me?" He said, "No, but I'll make you wish you were dead." God is not looking to kill anyone, but He will make some folks wish they were dead.

We have to reap what we have sown. If we have any complaints about the way our leaders are handling their business, we should complain about ourselves. We have created this generational curse. Here is something to think about: a lot of people in the baby-boomer generation are retiring now. The people who were dropped by the baby boomers are now in leadership. Still, some baby boomers hold key positions. How long will it be before the baby-buster generation will be in complete control? When they come in complete control, what will they have to offer generation X? When people truly get my point, they will start saying, "Come, Lord Jesus, come."

A generational curse comes about by the introduction of wrong ideas from a current generation to a future generation. These ideas are perpetuated through future generations. My daughter Candi has called me several times to ask me if a certain illness runs on my side of the family. I jokingly tell her that all the people on my side of the family were crazy. For some reason, she wasn't surprised the first time I told her that. Many doctors will ask this question when attempting to diagnose a certain type of malady. It does not matter what the problem is, or what category the problem falls under, the method of recovery is the same. The doctor is looking for generational curses as a means to diagnose a person's problem.

I wonder if people really know what they are saying when they say that the northern tribes of Israel are lost? We had to receive some valuable information from this generation to know what we know today. How would anyone have known about God if that were true? There are countless of people who are dead and gone who did not hear about the gospel of Jesus Christ. If there were no one to continue with the gospel message, we would not know anything about the gospel. I wouldn't be writing this book, you wouldn't be reading it, and we would probably be warring against each other. If a generation completely left the earth, how could anything be passed on to the next generation? How can a person say that he or she really knows the plan of God, then turn around and say that the ten tribes are lost?

If your leader is telling you that, don't leave the ministry; just tell him or her to call me. People who say that the tribes are lost are people who do not know who they are. It was not a coincidence that Africans were brought to the United States as slaves. Although the white people were evil and misleading, it was the will of God for us to be here. This is what God had to say in reference to generation curses:

"keeping mercy for thousands, forgiving iniquity and transgressions and sin, by no means clearing the guilty, visiting the iniquity of the father upon the children, and the children's children to the third, and the fourth generation."

After reading that scripture for several years, I begin to wonder why God spoke of the third and fourth generation. I wondered what happened to the fifth generation. There are those who consider a generation to be twenty years, and then there are those who consider a generation to be forty years. In the book of Genesis, God tells Abraham that his descendents would be in slavery for four hundred years. Then God tells him what would happen in that fourth generation, indicating that God considers one hundred years as a generation. God visited the iniquities of the fathers on the children to the third and fourth generation because that was all the time God needed to deal with the issues the people had. The main issue was idolatry. God judges people in a cathartic fashion rather than in condemnation.

The teaching of traditional preachers is that God is waiting for someone to mess up so He can bop them in the head. God is not interested in hurting people. He is interested in correcting people in an attempt to bring the best out of His people. It is a sad message when a preacher tells people to repent to keep from going to hell. During the time I was in an unregenerate state, this message would have meant nothing to me. I would have told the preacher to bring it on. I would have looked forward to the challenge of hell. I was one of those people who would have gone down there and installed air conditioners. After God deals with people for a few generations, people begin to get the message.

The United States is under God's judgment this very moment, and somebody is just not getting it right now. The economy that has been taken into captivity, countless number of people are hating on our black president, evangelicals are finding themselves with issues of being prejudice, and a few other maladies this nation face; they are God's attempt to get America back on her feet. God is not trying to destroy America. He is trying to employ America. America has the task of taking the gospel to the most remote areas of the earth. With the reputation America has at this time, it may be impossible to do. Looking at the leadership of today, and seeing how things are moving so far to the left, I wonder what the last generation leadership of this age will be like.

It's scary to even speculate. The president will be in late taking care of certain matters because he or she will be too busy playing his video games. Senators will be late convening because most of them are too busy on Facebook. Congressmen will find it difficult to assist the people in their districts because they were too involved with Korean women on MySpace. Although this is mere speculation, don't be surprised if you see TV trials of politicians facing charges for derelict of duty.

I was watching the news concerning the protests in Egypt. A partial speech from the president came on with the president stating that the United States was on top of things through the entire ordeal. After that, an ambassador came on and said that he disagreed with the president. Of course, we all have the right to disagree, but some things should go unsaid. It was a showing of the disunity and confusion in our country. It shows other nations the vulnerability of our nation. It lets the terrorist know the best time to make their attacks. A country divided against itself cannot stand, as Abraham Lincoln said.

If we are seeing these things happening now, what are we going to see ten years from now? My wife is concerned about our eighteen-year-old daughter. She has her own vehicle; she received $20,000 when she turned eighteen, and she has a boyfriend who has no job, did not finish school, and has nothing at all to bring to the table. My wife stated that she is experiencing grave disappointment with our daughter. She also stated that she is getting calls from other parents with worse concerns than the aforementioned one. There are a lot of teens and young adults doing the same thing. What will life be like when this generation takes the leadership? I am not saying that I'm not concerned with our daughter, but I have a different take on the matter. I told my wife that we trained our daughter well. She is doing things the way she's doing it because it gives her the upper-hand. She has the control. My daughter can manipulate him when she chooses to. She has the ability to take off with her girlfriends whenever she wants to.

She does not have to wait on him to take her places. I told my wife that our daughter has to run her course and experience the things we told her not to do for certain reasons. There will be those teens and young adults who will not learn the lessons for the prohibitions. It will be murder for our country when they end up in leadership. Many baby boomers have retired already, and by the year 2016, approximately another 50 percent would be retired. A few baby boomers are still in leadership, but it will not be enough to make a difference. My next concern with this new generation of leadership is the moral condition of our country. This part of the book will be met with much criticism and resentment.

We can apply the word *alternative* to so many categories that it is almost inevitable for conflict to arise. There is alternative lifestyles, alternative health, alternative relationship, alternative work ethic, and alternative, alternative, alternative. The word *alternative* has changed in meaning. It is a word that describes a person or a situation that allows one to remove the sting out of doing wrong. With so much ambiguity in our modern-day vernacular, it is imperative that I explain my position on the word *moral*. According to *Merriam-Webster's Dictionary*, moral means "of or related to conduct or character from the point of view of right and wrong." Based on a set of rules of right and wrong instituted by our Creator, the giver and ruler of life, there is a right and wrong way of doing and being.

Based on the attitude of our Creator, I draw my conclusions of the right and wrong way things are done. I must also make it clear that I'm not being judgmental or harsh toward those things I establish as wrong or the people who are doing them. I maintain a point of view that God is not in the condemning business but the construction business. God is more concerned with building his people as opposed to destroying his people. Based on that concept, I proceed with my approach to the wrongs of our society, and the possible dilemmas in which they may put us.

I start with homosexuality. God loves the homosexual just as much as He loves the heterosexual. God's love for His people is not based on merit. God's love is based on who and what He is. God is love. God's nature is love. God gave man the responsibility of replenishing the earth. What would happen if all the men decided to be homosexual? Human beings as we know would at some point become extinct. It takes a male and a female coming together to bring forth life. The reason God forbids people to be homosexual is for that very reason. The clergy has been too harsh in their approach toward homosexuals. It is wrong, but God is not sitting back adding points each time a homosexual act takes place. Our country is moving toward freedom for all. Although black people are moving closer to the freedom for which we fought for so long, as we near this freedom, we will find ourselves in a world of parallel freedom. People will be free to express themselves in any manner they see fit. I wonder if the day will come when people will be able to express themselves sexually in a public place without any type of recourse. When the door of opportunity opens, a lot of unexpected guesswork comes in.

The door is open. The time will come when people will want to close it, but it will be too late. The domino effect is now in place. One thing will lead to another, and when we look up, we will find ourselves in some places we would rather not be in. The problem with this is that, of course, it will be too late to turn back. If we take the time to look back to the times before terror attacks, the times before gay marriages, the times before prayer was taken out of schools, the time before the Ten Commandments were taken out of federal buildings, and so on, we will see a time when the United States experienced the most peace since its inception. When we look around today and see the moral decay of our country, we also see the parallel to that decay, which is the unrest we find ourselves in today.

It is befitting for me to wonder what the moral disposition of our country will be like in the years to come because I have children and grandchildren, and based on the way things are going today, I may even have some great-grandchildren. It is impossible to speculate on what is going to take place, but God's word provides us with the things to expect. Matthew 24, Mark 13, and Luke 21, give a vivid account of what to expect. There are quite a few things with hidden information. It gives us an indication but not a detailed explanation. I just know that it is a time when people will wish they had listened to the clergy.

In Matthew 24, Jesus admonishes us to learn the parable of the fig tree. To understand the parable of the fig tree is to understand that the current generation is the time when all the things Jesus spoke of will take place. One of the things I focus on in that chapter is the fact that Jesus says that many people will be offended. There are so many reasons to be offended during these days and times.

There is the question of racial discrimination lurking in my mind. We have been a divided country for a very long time. We have been able to conquer our enemies in the midst of this division. I think back to the time I first entered the military in 1973. Much discrimination existed during that time. After seeing the degree of discrimination, I was prompted to ask my father about his experience in World War II. He told me about the black army and the white army. He said the only time the two races were together was in the mess hall. I'll never forget the anger in his voice when he told me about the guy who said, "I don't see why we have to eat in here with these niggers."

I experienced a great deal of discrimination, so I know it was very tough for my father since he had probably experienced worse. I'm surprised he didn't teach me to be discriminative. I'm really glad he didn't. I had enough deficits to dig myself out of. Discrimination only facilitates the destruction of our country from within.

I believe the terror attacks were put on hold after the swearing in of a black president. The terrorists are smart enough to know the hatred that would stem from that selection. They are sitting back and observing. They figure we are about to destroy ourselves based on the track record of the United States. It certainly has been a problem in evangelical circles. I had to stop listening to many televangelists because of the hate they were communicating for a black president. Having a black president has added fuel to the fire of those who already were heated because of a black presence. The division may cause more damage now that we have a black president.

I have gone through some real challenges because of where I live. I live in a place where the white people are prejudice and the black people are jealous. The white people do all they can do to keep black people from progressing, and the black people who are too lazy to put forth any effort are glad they are doing it. I am about to embark on something great. I have had some lies told to me, seen some judges afraid to stand for truth, and witnessed a justice system that's darker than sin. I told a congregation one Sunday morning that according to the dense thicket of particulars, Job went through his ordeal for nine months. I then stated how the Bible tells us to go boldly to the throne of God. I shared with them how I told God that Job went through his ordeal for nine months; I have been going through mine for two years. Since Job got double, I wanted triple. I'm waiting on it.

CHAPTER

The Book of Revelations

I recall a noted comedian who had a joke concerning a scripture in the book of Revelations. He told of the part where John states that he saw a beast rising up out of the sea, having seven heads and ten horns, and on his horns, ten crowns, and on his heads, a blasphemous name. After repeating the scripture, he made the statement, "I don't know about you, but I don't want to see no mess like that." Many people read that particular scripture in the book of Revelations and get the image of something dangerous, scary, and something to be avoided if at all possible. It is all symbolic. The sea is equivalent to a multitude of people. The beast is equivalent to a system or the person of that system. The ten horns are the nations that will be over this system, and the crowns are representative of the authority of the ten nations.

The book of Revelations is a revelation of Jesus Christ. It is so stated in the beginning of the book. When the book of Revelations is viewed as a revelation of the end times, a lot of faulty interpretations result. If we keep in mind that it is the revelation of Jesus Christ, the interpretations will come out differently. I'll give an example: there is a part in the book that tells of how men will desire the rocks to fall on them and kill them. If one were to have in mind that the book is the revelation of the end time, one would get an image of some men standing at the bottom of a mountain praying that large rocks on the top of the mountain would fall down on them and kill them. If one was to ponder the feelings of the past years, one may think of a time when one wanted to commit suicide or wished to be dead.

We don't have to wait for a certain time in the future when this will happen. If one were to keep in mind that it is the revelation of Jesus Christ, one would see that it is an indication of the hardships involved with coming into the image of Jesus Christ. Sin put such an awful stain on humanity. It takes a lot of pain to be reconstructed to come into the image of Jesus Christ. A lot of what we read in the book of revelations is happening right now. I should get no argument concerning the condition the world is in today. It was not in this condition a few decades ago. The world is getting worse and worse as it pertains to any category one brings up. The moral fabric of our country has been depleted. I can write about some other categories, but I'm sure they are well-known by many people.

After reading the preceding paragraphs, one may get the idea that John went off on a tangent. To associate the book of Revelations with events in our lives would cause one to think that the book had nothing to do with the end-times. This is where we get into the law of double reference. A culmination of events will be associated with the tribulation period. The book speaks of the trumpets, the vials, and the bowls. There are some people who can testify that the book of Revelations reminds them of their current life. John was not going off on a tangent when he wrote of the events that pertain to the trumpets, vials, and bowls. We read in Revelation 17 and 18 about the fall of Babylon the great. One chapter speaks of the economic system, and the other speaks of the political and religious system.

As I wrote this section, I thought about how gas prices have risen. Banks' interest rates on their saving and money-market accounts are at a very low rate. The housing market has been turned upside down and inside out. The right side of the market has moved to the left, and the left side has moved all together. One may think that we are already in the tribulation period. There are notable ministers of the gospel who feel that the end is at the culmination of the year of 2012. I refuse to speculate on that matter.

There is a different rapture theorist who would have some real problems with that. The pre-tribulation theorist would say no way. The mid-tribulation theorist would say go away, and the end-tribulation theorist would say stay away. I believed in the rapture for many years. I am now in the middle on the matter. I couldn't care one way or the other.

I have gone through so much during my lifetime that it almost seems unfair not to be allowed to remain through such a time. It's like being on a football team: I practiced all week in the snow and the rain, with a bad knee, have been away from my family, been unable to eat any of my favorite foods, and then, on game day, Sunday, I have to sit on the bench. The training God has taken me through has pretty much prepared me for anything. It is amazing how so many people can look at one particular scripture and get so many different meanings. The only thing I can tell people is to wait and see. Many important things need to be done, and we should not spend our time arguing over doctrine. Some things are not that important.

If we are allowed to go through the tribulation, God will protect us as always. Let's take a look at the internal and external aspects of the book of Revelations. The internal aspect has to do with the events that take place in our lives. I'm sure that when some events took place in your life, you could not see God being involved in them. I know I have. It just seems that God's involvement would bring forth a better awareness, that one would have no problem knowing it was test time. It should be more like a test we took in college. It seems as if we should be aware that we are getting ready to take a test. For the most part, in college, we are aware that we are going to take a test. There are those exceptions when we get a pop quiz. Well, all of God's tests are pop quizzes.

The book of Revelations has been taught as an eschatological book as opposed to being the revelation of Jesus Christ. The book clearly states that it is the revelation of Jesus Christ. When we think of the seven trumpets, we see events that take place in our lives. God has to get those distractions out of us because they prevent us from walking in His love. I have heard of many ministers who stated that there was a time in their lives when they wanted to give up their faith. The fire of God will bring us to that point.

Many ministers dwell on the letter of the law when they teach and preach. They preach of how God is going to send them to hell if they don't do this, that, and the other thing. Preachers need to teach and preach on walking in the love of God. When a person walk is in the love of God, the desire to sin is demolished. Jesus says, "A new law I give you; love the Lord your God with all of your heart, and love your neighbor as yourself" (Matthew 22:37). It is the law of Love. The events we read about concerning the seven trumpets are events sent to destroy the works of the flesh. God is trying to kill the flesh, not the person. Happy is the man who makes it to the seventh trump, for he would then be like Christ."

I wrote the information on the preceding day around noon. When I turned on the television that evening to one of the church channels, I caught a person teaching about the seven trumpets. He taught that the first trump took place in World War I, the second took place in World War II, and the third trump took place at the Chernobyl explosion in the Ukranian SSR in 1986. I am not refuting what he said because, as I said earlier, many people view the book of Revelations as an account of end-time events.

I wrote earlier of the internal and external interpretation of revelations. Internally, a lot of the things are conducive to the events that take place in our lives. Externally, they are events that take place in our environment. Jesus says this: "My words are Spirit, and they are life." The Bible cannot be understood from an intellectual point of view. It is a spiritual book. The reason so many people err with its interpretation is due to the attempt to understand it through intellect. I have spoken with Muslims who say the book is contradictory. Muslims respect Jesus as a great prophet, but not as the Son of God. When the deity of Jesus is rejected, there is no filling of the Holy Spirit. It takes being filled with the Holy Spirit to be able to interpret the Bible.

When I heard the teaching that evening concerning the trumpets, I didn't have an opinion one way or the other. He may be right. It is imperative that we understand the internal interpretation of the book because it shows the way we develop. Jesus made some profound promises to him that overcomes. God is not playing a chess game with our lives. God has given man the freedom of choice. Some people choose to do evil things. The evil things they do have an effect on the people who are aspiring to walk in the love of God. It is not God's fault that people make the choices they make. God is looking for people who will love Him by choice, not by force. People feel the same way.

He only had time to teach on the first three. I initially decided to try to catch him the next week, when he would expound on the next four. But I changed my mind and chose not to wait a full week to hear the rest of the story. I ordered a downloadable version of the entire message. In Matthew 24:22, Jesus says something very interesting. Jesus says that unless those days were shortened, no one would be saved. He was referring to the events that would take place after the abomination of desolation takes place. That would be the time the Anti-Christ places himself in the temple and proclaim himself as God. Because of the things that are going to take place, it is going to be advantageous for the days to be shortened because people will endure less pain and hardship that way.

Some people teach that the days being shortened refers to the tribulation period being shortened. That could not be true because Bible prophecy cannot be altered. If what was prophesied concerning that particular time and event were to be changed, we would not know what to expect concerning any other prophecy in the Bible. The Bible would not be a reliable source. The days being shortened refers to the length of a day. According to the teaching I have been referring to, the man said that the fourth trumpet sounded in 1989 in relation to the Berlin Wall coming down. It was said that since this event, God has shortened the days. The man also said that the fifth trumpet sounded when Saddam Hussein burned the oil fields in Kuwait. The nation remained dark twenty-four hours a day for three months.

I decided to order more of this person's teaching materials. I must admit that he makes some strong points. I must still stick to the law of double reference when it comes to the events spoken of in the book of Revelations. The law of double reference in the book of Isaiah should be a way that gives the Bible student a better understanding of the law. It is prophesied in the book that a child is given, referring to the coming of Jesus Christ. It also spoke of a child that was born at that time. It should not be a hard thing to see where the law applies to the book of Revelations. There is so much more to understand about the book than what has been taught.

Revelations 2:17 speaks of hidden manna. No one really knows exactly what it's like, at least no one on the earth today. The best that I could get from the biblical description is that it is similar to sweet bread. It was given to the children of Israel during their visit in the desert. God gave it to them as a means of sustaining life. It is representative of how Jesus Christ sustains our life. Jesus says that he was the bread of life. I felt the need to include the book of Revelations in this book because of the law of double reference. Many people's children are out of control due to the events in their lives that have caused them pain. That is why it is necessary for me to write this book as to explain that pain.

After doing some extensive research concerning the hidden manner Jesus spoke of, I came to the conclusion that no one really knows what it is. I write out the verse—Revelations 2:17—as a means of showing why I think no one knows:

"He, who has an ear, let him hear what the Spirit says to the churches. To him who overcomes I will give some of the hidden manner to eat. And I will give him a white stone, and on the stone a new name written which no one knows except him who receives it. Only those who have overcome can know what it is, and they are not around to tell us. There is one thing I know; coming from Jesus it has to be excitingly good.

Overcoming hardships entails understanding why one's children are out of control. Without this understanding, it is impossible to get them under control. Those inner children that causes a wife to not be romantic with her husband because of the incest or molestation she experienced could come under control once she understands her reactions and begins to apply the principles necessary to overcome those unwanted reactions. Those inner children that are in people who have been rejected all of their lives and make forming relationships difficult could overcome their issues by their understanding why they had this experience and applying the principles accordingly.

Those inner children in the person who was emotionally abused can be overcome by understanding the reason for the emotional abuse, and applying the necessary principles that will allow him or her to respond to life according to principles as opposed to responding out of their emotions. Those inner children in the people who were physically abused and think that it is okay to be in a relationship in which there is physical abuse. Women who were physically abused and who think that a man doesn't love her unless he is hitting her must wake up. They need to understand that there is a much better life than what they are experiencing.

Because I am dealing with emotions, I have to do a parenthetical passage right here. The first book I wrote was titled *Why "U" Do the Things "U" Do*. I told a person I studied with and spoke for at some of her meetings that I had completed my book concerning emotions. Her response was that she was not going to read my book if I didn't have anything in it about nutrition. It is true that one's emotional state can be affected by nutrition, but not on the level I write and speak on. (I consume a nutritional coffee and tea that provides an excellent way to take in the nutrition the body requires. The products are found at *www.bpatterson.organogold.com*. It is especially a good source for those who are already coffee consumers.)

I use the book of Revelations because of the law of double reference. It allows people to understand the reason for the turmoil in their lives. Again, when John introduces the book of Revelations, he states that it is the revelation of Jesus Christ. He speaks of the method God uses to reveal Jesus Christ in the believer.

There are so many different teachings concerning the book of Revelations. There are those who do not believe in the rapture. I read a book in which the author stated how it would not make any sense for God to allow a believer to go through the tribulation period. It is a point well taken. I don't believe the external events will take place in the entire world. I came to the conclusion that it is not beneficial to anyone to argue over doctrine. I decided to not even teach on the rapture. This is how I see it: if we are raptured up, fine; if not, still fine. Either way, God is going to protect His people.

There are those who teach that Revelation 4:1 is a picture of the rapture. They also teach that the book of Revelations is written in chronological order. A close look at the book will help one to see the reason I say it is not written in chronological order. There are those who teach that Revelations 1 is history. It shows that chapters 2 and 3 were the present, and chapters 4 through 22 are the future. It is also taught that the seven trumpets are confined to a future seven-year period.

Such teaching throws off the time frame in which things will take place. One of the things that will allow the Bible student to see the spiritual aspect of the book is to understand the difference between the wrath of Satan and the wrath of God. The wrath of Satan takes place the last three-and-a-half years of Daniel's seventieth week. The wrath of God takes place at the end of the seven-year period. Jesus comes at the seventh trumpet. He pours out the vials at His coming. The wrath of Satan is carried out with hatred being his motivation. God's wrath is poured out as a means of repentance. God use the suffering of His saints to build us into the image of His son Jesus.

The apostle Paul says, "[T]hat I may know Him in the power of His resurrection and the fellowship of His suffering." Jesus Christ suffered to the extent of death on a cross. It was the most compunctious way a person could suffer. God said that it pleased Him to bruise His son. If it pleased Him to bruise His son, where does that leave us? Those things mentioned in the scrolls, trumpets, and vials are conducive to the suffering we experience today as Christians. That is why it is dangerous to teach people that after they accept Jesus Christ as their savior, everything is going to be all right all the time. Many people will testify that they had more problems after they were saved.

If one were to carefully study the seals, trumpets, and vials, one would find that there are parallels among them. It is believed by some that the sixth seal, the seventh trumpet, and the seventh vial are all the same. In studying it myself, I cannot refute that teaching. With the three paralleling each another, it takes us to a post–rapture forum. The thing that went along with that teaching was that all who went to heaven had to be beheaded for their faith. I don't agree with that. It also says in the Bible that God will keep us out of the hour of temptation. I believe that those who are saved during the tribulation will be beheaded for their faith. It would rob us all of our hope if we only had beheading to look forward to.

Jesus says that the tribulation will be a time that has never been nor ever will be. If we were to take a look at the patriarchs after the death, burial, and resurrection of Jesus Christ, we find some very grating persecutions such as being beheaded, being hung upside down on a cross, being boiled in oil, and other detestable occurrences. Jesus says that the tribulation period will be worse than that. I expect this book to be completed by the year 2012.

God is getting ready to lavish His blessings on the saved population as a means of showing the nonbelievers who He is. People are going to know beyond the shadow of a doubt that He is in fact God, the creator of the universe. In this time of economic meltdown, God's people will be prospering beyond comprehension. I believe that if it is correct that Christians must go through the tribulation, God will bestow on Christians unparalleled benefits as a means to convince those who were not convinced prior to the tribulation period. John says that he saw a number that could could not be the number who go to heaven. They were of all tongues, kindred, people, and nations. Many will be convinced by the life of the righteous during that time.

One should read the sixth seal and compare it to the seventh trumpet along with the vials. In Matthew 24:29, Jesus says that after the tribulation of those days, the moon will be darkened, the sun will not give its light, and the stars will fall from heaven. This is an indication that positions of the three different rapture theories should be considered for further study. In the book of Daniel, it is stated that the prophecy of this book is sealed until the end.

We will take a look at the 144,000 mentioned in the book of Revelations. After John mentions the 144,000, he then states that he saw a multitude that no one could number, of all nations, tribes, peoples, and tongues. Just before, John states that he saw another angel, ascending from the east, with the seal of the living God. The angel cries with a loud voice to the four angels to whom harming the earth and the sea were granted. He said, "Do not harm the earth, the sea, or the trees until we have sealed the servants of our God on their foreheads" (Revelations 7:2–9).

I believe the 144,000 is a representation of the number that no one could number. John took time out to name each tribe and its size. God tells Abraham that all nations of the earth would be blessed through him. We see in the aforementioned scripture that all nations are represented. Something else should be mentioned here. After Cain kills his brother, God pronounces a curse on him. Cain retorts to God that anyone who finds him will kill him. God sets a mark on Cain that prevents anyone from killing him. It is possible that the 144,000, being a representation of all nations, kindred, tongues, and people, will be sealed in the same manner.

I know this is an unpopular account, but one must keep in mind what the prophet Daniel said. Daniel states that the prophecy of this book is sealed until the time of the end. We are now in the end-times. Every minister I know and listen to concurs with that notion. In the midst of two or three witnesses, let a word be established. I was reading one man's perspective on the subject, and he stated that to tell Christians that the rapture will not take place prior to the tribulation period is robbing Christians of hope. Whether the rapture takes place before the tribulation or whether we will be protected through that period, we can still remain hopeful.

CHAPTER

Why So Much Pain?

I'm sure there are countless of Christians asking the question, "Why so much pain?" The fall of man is a good place to start with the question. Adam and Eve were self-sufficient after creation. It wasn't until the fall that they begin to have challenges. They had such a wonderful life, which was derived from a wonderful relationship with God. The devil was able to convince Eve that there was more to life than they were experiencing. He stirred up Eve's curiosity. Eve did not have anything to which to compare life. She didn't realize that she had the best thing going. If there were other people around who were struggling with life, Eve would have found out why they were struggling.

Once she found out the reason, she would have told that serpent to go to hell where he belonged. Eve had no idea of the freedom she had. As a result of her wanting to know what she was missing out on, she decided to buy into the lie she had been told. Adam had the power to stop sin from entering in the earth, had he made the right decision. This shows the influence women have over men. Because of Adam's decision, sin entered into the world. God had given Adam instructions prior to Eve's entry on the earth, telling him that the day he sinned, he would die. Man was supposed to live forever.

The first death Adam and Eve suffered was a spiritual death. It took a long time for them to die physically, but eventually, it happened. The death God was referring to was the separation from Him. When this took place, man had to go back to the drawing board. Restoring something to its original state is a long and arduous process. Not only is the process timely and difficult; it is also painful. It was not God's choice to do things this way. God knew which decision Adam would make and had already had a plan in place to reconcile man back to Himself, which is stated in Genesis 3:15. It is the first prophecy concerning Jesus Christ.

Sin entering the earth gave birth to many maladies we can now find ourselves affected by. There are those who think that the catastrophes we suffer from today are a result of God's judgments. I once thought this myself and could have put in some of my writings. After a better understanding of the dispensation of grace, I had to change my view on the matter. It is not time for God's judgments. The Bible tells us that the earth itself is groaning and waiting for that same time of peace that we are waiting for. Sin caused everything to go sour. It caused a lot of people to sour.

There are countless of adults who are dealing with childhood issues. There are adults who would like to change their behavior but do not have a clue as to how to do so. There are those who have personality disorders but have decided to get comfortable with them. There are those who are afraid of change. For some people I've come in contact with, I must say that change is good. Too many people are ashamed of their true self and would rather keep it hidden from others as much as possible. Hidden issues will always remain issues. Effort is needed to bring forth change. Change for many is difficult, and hiding the issues is their best avenue for peace. Change can also be very painful.

To bring forth change one must get to the root of the problem. One can start by looking at the categories that all issues fall under. There is emotional abuse, physical abuse, rejection, incest, and molestation. One must look back over his or her life and determine what was prevalent in their life from childhood to the present. It is believed that rejection is the worst case of all. I tend to agree with that because I know the pain. It is painful to find out how we were affected, especially if we were proud of our parents. To find out that the way we were raised brought on a lot of our issues could be very devastating to many of us.

When one can look back and figure out what was prevalent in his or her life, one would then be able to gauge the area in which change would need to take place. There is an innate need for people to have a sense of belonging. When a person can look back and see that he or she has a track record of rejection, one would then be able to trace the root to the those behaviors that are unwanted. Rejection can lead to such things as loss of respect, fear of knowledge, anger, bitterness, and so on. People who find that they are behaving in ways that are connected to these types of issues can then start the process to recovery.

One must also see the Bible as the manual that governs life. The principles necessary for recovery are found in it. There is a scripture in the Bible that tells us that we were blessed with all spiritual blessings. There are nine spiritual blessings. One of them is the blessing of acceptance. People suffering from rejection must realize that they are accepted by the author of life. The fact that we are accepted allows us to be less concerned with those who do not accept us. Along with this idea, we must pay attention to what Jesus said in the gospels. Jesus said that we would have whatever we say.

That is why it is imperative that we have a daily faith confession. Every day, a rejected person should verbally say a verse that deals with acceptance. We can have things in our mind, yet they may not be in our spirit. It must reach our spirit in order to convince our mind that it is true. Many of us have experienced going into a grocery store or department store where music is being played. We were not really paying attention to the music, but hours later, we may find ourselves singing or humming the tune that we heard in the store. The music registered in our conscious. The faith confession works on that same concept.

Traditional Bible teaching has served the church a terrible blow. Within the black church community is a big problem regarding tradition. A lot of the preachers and teachers who lived during the Great Depression taught a lot of things out of ignorance. Education for black people wasn't as prevalent at that time as it was at later times. These preachers are in their seventies and beyond. With education not being available at that time for black people, think about the generation of black people before them. That generation didn't do the Depression generation any justice.

That generation had even fewer opportunities to be educated. So much guesswork was handed down. The Depression generation had an elementary understanding of the word. My destiny was nearly destroyed because of the bogus beliefs of teachers from this generation. This is not a smack in the face to those of this generation; they did the best they could with what they had. This generation did not know God the way they thought they did. We must really learn God's ways. A good example of this would be to look at the way Jesus suffered. The suffering of Jesus is made clear in the book of Isaiah.

Jesus was wounded for our transgressions, not His own. He didn't have any. I have seen so many angry teenagers and young adults. The sad thing about their situation is that they do not understand why they are angry. A lot of them don't even realize that they are angry. To know God is to know why we experience the tragedies we go through in life. God doesn't allow such tragedies because he is angry with us. He didn't allow His son Jesus to suffer because He was angry with Him. All of His sufferings had meaning and a purpose, just as ours do. We must learn the reason for our sufferings. To do so would open a new and exciting chapter in our lives.

The thing that got me started on childhood issues and the way they affected us as adults, has to do with what I learned from Dr. I. V. Hilliard. Since 1999, I have been diligently studying the subject. When I learned why I was the way I was, I became angry with my father. My father had passed on to glory the year before. It took an entire year for me to lose the anger. I did a lot of learning during that time. My studies of psychology and Christian counseling added a new dimension to what I had understood previously. I stated in another book that psychology did not provide the answers for life's problems, but it offered an excellent framework for a deeper study.

The answers for life's problems are found in the Bible. For instance, here is one of Abraham Maslow's hierarchies of needs: self-actualization, the need to reach our fullest potential. It is true that we have a need to reach our fullest potential, but psychology does not teach how to do that. To reach one's fullest potential is to walk in one's God-given purpose. Psychology doesn't get that deep; it only plays in shallow water. If it came out to the deep water, where Christianity is, it would drown. God trains all of us for our purpose. Many people don't realize they are going through God's training. That is why many end up angry and bitter. Angry people need to ask God why they had the experience they had in life.

God would be more than glad to explain it. I could not know what I know or do what I do had I not had the experience I had. I'm glad for my experiences. It didn't feel good at the time, but it is very rewarding now. This is the message I would like to give to angry people. Some people expect God to be a God who prevents us from experiencing any pain. God said that it pleased Him to bruise His Son. I know that sounds very harsh, but it was the only way God could reconcile humanity back unto Himself. It is stated in the Bible that Jesus is the first fruit of many sons. That means that God is pleased to also bruise the many sons. Jesus Christ was our example of what God expects from us.

The baby-boomer generation did a great disservice to the baby buster's generation. The baby boomers haven't put the care into children as those of the Great Depression generation did. Those from the baby-boomer generation did not want to be burdened down with child-rearing. There are always the few who are exceptions to the rule, but for the most part, the baby boomer generation was a generation of hippies, partygoers, and very selfish people. As a result, many children grew up with issues that followed them into adulthood. Although the baby boomers were a shiftless generation, those who are now living godly lives possess an unprecedented faith. The faith level of the Depression generation pales in comparison to that of these baby boomers.

It takes a far greater level of faith to deal with the perilous times we now live in. The world has changed drastically for the worst. People in the United States are working hard to get God out of our country. The problems we are facing now have everything to do with the disrespect our country has shown toward God. If the citizens of United States refuse to repent, the nation will continue to go downhill.

I listen to the commentators talk very negatively about our president while making suggestions on what he should be doing. I have not heard one person address the spiritual condition of our country. Everything they say is the wrong answer. I was listening to a one-on-one discussion between a news anchor and one of the wealthiest people in our nation. The person stated that the president should not be out campaigning; he should be behind his desk fixing the problems we are facing. It let me know how ignorant this person is. The person is so ignorant that he doesn't even know why he has what he has. He employs thousands of people. God called him for that reason, but he does not have enough sense to know it. He actually thinks his financial smarts have him in the position that he is in. The only reason he continues with the financial status he maintains is due to the godly people in his employment.

If the people in his company were like him, they would have been in the unemployment line some time ago. It is the faith of the godly people in the United States that are carrying this nation. The baby boomers are exercising unprecedented faith that is holding things where they are. We must really prepare for kingdom living at this time. The name of my church is Kingdom Living Training Center. What I'm about to say would probably be refuted by many evangelicals. I wrote in a previous book, *Don't Lose Your Head*, that there will not be any more white presidents. There are many evangelicals who believe that the church will be raptured prior to the tribulation period. It has been taught that way for so many years.

Consider this: in the book of Daniel, God tells Daniel that the things he inquires of are sealed until the times of the end. Daniel remains quite inquisitive. God tells Daniel to shut the book and to go somewhere and just chill out. He also tells Daniel that he is trying to know too much. The teachings from fifty to one hundred years ago were the teachings from a sealed book. Now that we are in the end-times, knowledge has increased as indicated in the book of Daniel. Those who hold tight to the traditional teaching will not be open-minded enough to receive the truth.

One of the first times I recall a mention of a tribulation period, it was called the time of Jacob's trouble. I heard a minister on television assert that the church is not the house of Jacob. Indulge me for just a moment. The Assyrians took the ten northern tribes of Israel into captivity. After their captivity, they migrated to the Caucasus Mountains, from which the word *Caucasian* is derived. These same Caucasians continued their migration to northern and northwestern Europe. Daniel 7:4 says: "The first was like a lion and had eagles' wings. I watched till its wings were plucked off. It was lifted up from the earth and made to stand on two feet like a man, and a man's heart was given to it." The lion is the symbol of Great Britain, and the eagle is the symbol of the United States.

Many people came to the Americas from Great Britain. The first prophecy of the United States is found in the book of Genesis. Genesis 48:14–20 shows the United States and Great Britain. The United States is the great nation, and Great Britain is the multitude of nations. Scripture clearly proves that the church is the house of Jacob. Besides, it doesn't take a rocket scientist to see how the United States has turned its back on God. It is amazing as we go through this economical meltdown how the analysts attempt to show how our president is wrong in the approach he takes to resolve our nation's crisis. All of those smart politicians who think they know how to fix the problem are just as wrong as two left shoes.

The solution to our problem is found in 2 Chronicles 7:14: "If my people who are called by name, will humble themselves and pray, turn away from their wicked ways, and seek my face, then will I hear from heaven, and then will I heal your land." I have not heard one smart politician say that. Many of them are still upset about a black man being president. They don't say it publicly, but we know what is said behind closed doors. Having a black president marks the start of a new era called Jacob's troubles. It started three-and-a-half years after President Barack Obama took office. I'll talk briefly about Jonathan's harbingers.

In Isaiah 9:10, we read of the nine ways Israel defied God. God sent warnings to Israel to get the nation back on track. God allowed the Assyrians to overtake Israel. In doing so, many buildings were torn down, along with some of the valued terrain. Israel decided to defy God by not repenting and spoke of how she would rebuild. On September 11, 2001, God allowed the terrorists to destroy the World Trade Center towers. The United States took the same route the Israelites of antiquity took. The same decisions were made that was made earlier. One person actually quoted Isaiah.

During my visit to New York, I saw for myself the evidence of our nation's defiance. It is amazing how the chapel, which was so close to the wreckage, came out unscathed. It is the same chapel where George Washington dedicated our nation to God. I know there are those who would say it is only coincidental, but they will get the revelation soon enough. When the Israelis of antiquity defied God after the Assyrian attack, a calamity hit that nation every seven years. Is it coincidence that seven years after the towers went down we had the economic meltdown? In September 2001, the towers went down. In September 2008, the economy went down. What's going down in September 2015?

Maybe someone will agree with me that we must learn to live according to kingdom principles. As I think about the three levels of Christianity, which are Passover, Pentecost, and Tabernacle, I have to marvel. The church has operated on level two for much too long. It operates on the Pentecostal level of speaking in tongues and prophesying. There is nothing wrong with that, but there is something incomplete with that. I heard Myles Munroe put it this way: "The church is doing nothing more than having memorial services." I have to agree with him because the church as a whole is not teaching kingdom living. Too much teaching focuses on matters that doesn't move the church forward. We need kingdom principles, not church principles. I was born into the kingdom, not into the church.

Passover represents one's initial birth into the kingdom. Pentecost represents the baptism into the Holy Spirit. There are Bible teachers and preachers who say that everything a believer gets, he or she gets at the time of acceptance of Jesus Christ. Let me show that to be as asinine as someone who tries to fry ice cream. When the apostle Paul approached the new believers, he asked them had they received the Holy Ghost since they believed. The response was that they had not as much as heard of the Holy Ghost. This question was addressed to believers and followers of Jesus Christ. There are Bible teachers today who are not baptized in the Holy Spirit. I do not waste my time listening to them. The Holy Spirit will teach us all things. Think about it.

I had to mention that for those who have been infected by such foolish teachings. Once one began to operate on tabernacle level, all the foolish tradition goes out the door. Fear goes out the door; ungodly jealousy goes out the door; unforgiveness goes out the door; resentment, hatred, racism, and the like goes out the door. One operates in total obedience at this level. I had to stop listening to so many Caucasian ministers and pastors after President Obama was elected. Think about this: the president of the United States has always been considered the most powerful man in the world. Now a man who is considered to be ignorant and inferior is the most powerful man in the world.

There are many pastors and ministers of the Caucasian persuasion who never had the real challenge of racism. For so many years, black people were in positions of subjugation. There was the absence of the challenge to racism. Now the challenge is there. Many pastors and ministers found out that they really didn't know themselves. When they preach and teach, we can hear their racism coming out. Some are not racist. They are the ones who operate on the tabernacle level. God is so good that He allows these others to see themselves. It is a struggle for many, but we are praying that they pull through. There is so much peace on the tabernacle level. The fact still remains, though: a new level, a new devil.

While the ministers strive for the tabernacle level, the church as a whole must do so also. The church needs to move up to the tabernacle level because that is the level of obedience. Jesus commanded believers to preach the gospel of the kingdom. The church is preaching the gospel of the church.

A lot of the Depression-generation ministers and pastors were taught things that are not biblical, and they are closed-minded to the real teachings and revelations. Many pastors who have been in ministry for forty years or more find it difficult to change their belief system. It is very difficult for anyone who has been doing or believing something for forty or more years to change. There are pastors of antiquity who think that the baby-boomer generation ministers and pastors are out in left field. We cannot be concerned with what they think. We must preach the gospel of the kingdom.

Kingdom Aspects

The Bible tells us that the kingdom of God is righteousness, peace, and joy in the Holy Spirit. Along with that, Jesus says that the kingdom of God is within. I will not attempt to exhaust a complete detail of kingdom aspects, but I will deal with the prerequisites.

The Bible lists three aspects of the kingdom, and I deal with these aspects. We must understand what these aspects entail as a means to understanding them. Because we are dealing with tabernacle-level Christianity, it must be noted that this level calls for great faith. Because the kingdom of God is within, we must possess the three aspects within. Maintaining those characteristics within takes great faith. The reason for such great faith is found in Matthew 24:7 and 10.

In Matthew 24:7, Jesus says that nation will rise against nation and kingdom against kingdom. I've never known it in the way it's happening now. Iran is talking about blowing Israel off the map and attacking the United States on its own soil. Russia says it will not sit idly while Iran fights the United States. This means that all the allies of the countries will get involved. In the book of Revelations, it talks about war that would kill one third of the earth's population.

It sounds like World War III to me. Also, Jesus says that kingdom will rise against kingdom. "Kingdom" here equates to ethnic groups. An ethnic group can consist of mixed races. It can also consist of one race. There's the Klu Klux Klan, who I believe later changed their name to the Tea Party. Homosexuals are demanding their rights to have their relationships be legal. There are other groups, but the point is that these groups are knitted together because of one common thread of anger. The groups that are of opposite race are rising up against one another like never before. One reason is due to the inauguration of a black president.

Many people are angry because the United States has had 234 years of white presidents, and they can't understand what happened. This group also includes the Caucasians of the Christian community. Along with the other things, Jesus mentions that these will be the beginning of sorrows. After more horrific descriptions, Jesus says that there will be great tribulation. The definition of *sorrow* is distress or suffering from oppression or persecution. Tribulation is distress because of an unpleasant state. Jesus is saying that this is the beginning of the tribulation period.

In Matthew 24:14, Jesus says that this gospel of the kingdom will be preached in the entire world as a witness to all the nations, and then the end will come. According to Paul Crouch, founder of Trinity Broadcasting Network (TBN), this has taken place. God has used Paul and Jan to do an awesome work in the earth. I was watching behind the scenes when I saw Paul and his son broadcasting from Jerusalem. They were dedicating the new satellite they were finally able to put in Israel. I believe Paul stated that he had been praying for nearly thirty years for God to allow him to put a satellite in Israel. God could not answer his prayer initially because the timing was not appropriate.

God had a set time as to allow Paul to put it in Jerusalem. It is my opinion that Israel is God's time element. When God does something with the nation of Israel, it signifies what God is doing in the earth. Paul Crouch placing a satellite in Israel has great significance. I believe it has to do with Matthew 24:14. It is the signpost that a prophesied event has been fulfilled. God has prepared many people for this time. He trained us through what I call trib junior—smaller tests of faith. So many of us have had many trials and test, and we watched as God delivered us from them all. God had to prove to us that He could take care of us. We started with tiny, to medium, to large, to extra large to wanting to commit suicide, but God!

As an expository of what the kingdom of God was all about, Jesus likens it to a mustard seed. It is amazing how Jesus uses the smallest seed of all to explain the kingdom. I think it parallels how God uses the simple things to confound the wise. I'm reminded at this point of an account in the book of Samuel. Samuel is given a mandate by God to anoint the next king. He is instructed to go to Jesse's house to find him. He looks at all of Jesse's sons except David, who is out in the field tending sheep. Jesse directs Samuel as he seeks out his choice for the future king to the most appealing sons he has and has no thought of mentioning David, a young fellow at the time.

After Samuel goes through all of Jesse's sons, he tells Jesse that they do not qualify. Samuel even attempts to anoint one of them, but as he tries to pour out the oil, the Bible says that the oil stays in the flask although there is no obstruction. The power of our Almighty God prevents it from coming out. Samuel asks Jesse if he has another son he has not seen. Jesse tells him about David but talks about David in a negative way. Samuel instructs Jesse to send for him. David came in the house, and Samuel anoints him as the next king of Israel. David did not look like much to them, but he was God's next king.

According to the parable of the mustard seed, Jesus is saying that God will use the people we reject and will cause them to go beyond anyone could ever imagine. No one can see the seed that God planted in us. Not only did God plant a seed in us; He also set His kingdom up for us to do the same. Seed planting falls into many different facets, such as finances, friendship, marriage, and so on. We must plant what we would like to have. In the parable of the mustard seed, the harvest overshadows the seed. God's way of counting is so much different from man's ways of counting.

I hope no one is offended by what I have to say about the stock market. I know some really influential men of God deal with it. This is just my opinion of the market; I am in no way trying to carve this concept into stone. The Bible directs kingdom people to stay away from the world's system. I was going to get involved with the stock market at one time. This was before the meltdown, of course. I started thinking that the stock market worked on the same principle as the kingdom. I believe the difference in the market being or not being the world system would be the type of people in control of the market. I believe that if a group of evangelicals who loved God had come together and formed a stock market, it would be different.

People who love God will not rob people. People who love God will fulfill the law by walking in the love of God. Jesus says that He fulfilled the law. This is why he was able to give us a new commandment: "Love the Lord thy God, and love your neighbor as yourself." This means that a person who does not love God cannot love himself or herself, nor can they love others. I know there are those who do not believe in God but claim they love people. I didn't say they could not have affection for others. There is a distinct difference. Affection has to do with feelings alone whereas love has to do with making a choice. Affection could go along with love, but love can never be affection only.

A group of people who walk in a genuine love and who manage a system similar to that of the stock market could operate under the same principles and not be considered the world system. What makes the stock market the world system are the people who control it. That is the reason so many people lost money in the fourth quarter of 2008. The time has come to where we must work the principles of the kingdom. We must plant seeds in the ministries that we know are fulfilling the great commission. It is vital to come into the knowledge of the kingdom. The Bible tells us to grow up and to be children only in malice. We must get our children under control now because it is a lot later than many people think.

There are kingdom principles that must be applied that would bring us the results we would like to have in life. I was invited to dinner the other day, and after dinner, we sat around the table and fellowshipped for a while. We were sharing nuggets of wisdom. A pastor, whom I had just met that day, spoke of the pride and the ego that went along with people who had issues but were covering them up. I agreed with him wholeheartedly, but I had to add the pain these people were experiencing. I spoke of the childhood experiences that were painful for us, and as a means of escaping that pain, we mask our past. Pride comes in at the point of us not wanting anyone to know what's going on in the inside.

People who are in leadership do not want their subordinates to know what is going on with them. The thinking is that if they knew what the inside of me looked like, they would not want me to be their leader. The ironic thing about the situation is that we are really hiding from each other. It is if we all are at a costume party. Some will be wearing a Zorro mask, some will have on a Batman mask, some will have on a Catwoman mask, and some will have on a Lone Ranger mask, and so on. We all will pretend to be having a wonderful time while drinking enough booze to kill a horse. We all have a lot of the same issues, but pride causes us to mask it all. Instead of being healed, we spend years playing hide and go seek.

The pain of the issues is so extensive that we would rather hide as opposed to dealing with the pain. We hide for many years attempting to avoid the pain. The sad thing about it is that the pain keeps us from confronting the issues. If we do not confront the issues, we cannot conquer the issues. We may end up not enjoying the kingdom life that God has purposed us to live. We must allow the child inside to grow up. We must become mature saints in the kingdom of the most-high God to live lives like kings and priests. There is an account in the Bible in which a king takes the throne at eight years old. He had seasoned advisers, and he had unseasoned advisers. He refused to heed the advice of the seasoned advisors and took the advice of the unseasoned advisors. I guess it doesn't take rocket science to figure the outcome. That's right, he made one gigantic mess. This is why it is imperative that we confront our issues and allow the children inside us to grow up. In this time of early tribulation, we must live by kingdom principles to survive. One of the ways of understanding kingdom aspects is to look at the example that God presents. God has many positions; one of those positions is God the father. We must look at God's role as God the father, God our provider. He is our protector, He is our teacher, and He is our nurturer.

As fathers, we have a serious obligation toward our children. A father is capable of representing one of two types of entities. A father can represent The God of Abraham, Isaac, and Jacob, or he can represent the God of the Pharisees. Jesus told the Pharisees that they were of their father the devil. In 2 Corinthians 5:20, it says that we are ambassadors of Christ. Also,

Jesus gives us a few parables to explain what the kingdom of God is like. In one parable, He talks about planting a mustard seed and how the smallest seed end up bringing the greatest harvest. Jesus also gives us parables concerning the kingdom of heaven. It should be understood here that there is a distinct difference in the kingdoms.

The kingdom of God refers to God's way of doing things. The kingdom of heaven is God's physical address. That's why the kingdom of heaven parables are different from the kingdom of God parables. The father plants seeds in his children. An absent father plants seeds, and a father that's present plant seeds. Both can plant good and bad seeds in their children. A father that beats his wife will have an effect on a child that will bring adverse ramifications. The five areas of pain would be a good way to explain my point. We'll take a look at molestation, rape, rejection, physical abuse, and emotional abuse.

The sexual sins, molestation and rape, cause people to have very low self-esteem. There are feelings of guilt and shame. People in this condition often do not qualify as good leaders. The thing that makes a good leader is attitude. One's attitude will be determined by the way one sees one's self. People in this condition find it very difficult to see themselves as being a great leader. A father who violates his children in this manner causes grave damage to his children. The seed the father plants grows into something that has to be seriously reckoned with. It would be very difficult to recover from such pain. I will in no way say that it can't be overcome, but it will not be a walk through the tulips.

The people affected in this manner will find it difficult to exercise the principles of the kingdom. The father is the ambassador to his children. He represents God in his home. These children grow up thinking that God is like their father. They may even go as far as to hate God. It is almost certain they would if they hate their father. The wound these people carry will make them mask the problem. They have no way of being healed without the knowledge of God's word. These people spend countless dollars in a psychiatrist's and/or a psychologist's office. The sad part about that scenario is that these professionals will attempt to assist these people with scientific means.

Psychology is the scientific study of human behavior. The psychologist can only deal with the mind while the spirit continues to suffer. The spirit has a wound that is so deep only God can reach it. God said that He sent His word to heal us. The psychologist does not use the word of God. I'm reminded of one of my psychology teachers telling of a study that determined that elderly people who were active with church were more content than were elderly people who had no church affiliation. The real reason is cause and effect. Psychology cannot say cause and effect because it would put a lot of people out of business.

The word *correlation* takes the sting out of cause and effect. Correlation merely means having a mutual relationship with something whereas cause and effect means that this happened because I did that. The elderly people were content because they were in the word of God. God's word is the only way the aforementioned people can be healed and delivered. The reason these people take so long, or never get healed is due to the pain. If I were fighting, and the person I was fighting stabbed me in the thigh, I would concentrate my attention on the wound. He may be beating me, but I'm going to be more concerned with the stab wound. I am too wounded to focus on the real problem so I just cover it up.

It is the same thing with emotionally wounded people. We are too wounded to focus on the real root of the problem, so we cover it up by wearing a mask. The problems we experience in life are perpetuated by our inability to deal with the pain. We portray ourselves as something we are not. If we are in a leadership position, the last thing we want is to allow our subordinates to see our weaknesses. We go many years wearing the mask. The problem with that is that we will never know our true selves. We will be unacquainted with the purpose we were created for. We respond to challenges with an emotional response, but it's always the wrong response.

The shame we experience in our lives will not allow us to be honest with our feelings. The shame keeps us from sitting down and talking with a good Christian counselor, such as me, to release our true feelings. The thing or things that we are not able to confront, we are not able to conquer. Our society has set such stringent expectations regarding how we should conduct ourselves that it causes people to hide their true self. No one wants to be looked at by society as a person who does not measure up. It starts with childhood when young people experience so much peer pressure. A lot of people are afraid to be different. The Bible tells us that we are a peculiar people, a royal priesthood.

We have a propensity to believe who society says we should be rather than who God says we are. There are people who believe in Jesus but are afraid to share their faith. They are afraid of being rejected. Rejection is the next painful area. Rejection is the main reason people will do whatever it takes to fit in. Women who are afraid of being rejected end up having children who were not planned. These children go through childhood without a father in their lives. There are various adverse ramifications that result from rejection. The five areas of pain make it impossible to operate the principles of the kingdom.

Physical abuse and emotional abuse have its place as kingdom principal preventers. It is imperative at this time in life to be able to operate according to the kingdom. There has been a shift in the earth. Things will not go back to the way they were. At the time of this writing, the presidential candidates are campaigning for the presidency. They are making promises that they will make everything better. They are very critical of our current president by stating how the economy is not getting any better. Neither our current president, nor any future president, cannot make this economy go back to what it used to be. Those days are gone forever. The next good thing we have to look forward to is Jesus setting up His kingdom.

I'm sure there are people who would like to know by what authority I can say there has been a shift. My wife and I have a friend who went to Japan to visit her daughter, who is married to a soldier stationed there. After being there for approximately a week, she called and said she was thrown off when she had her money changed over. She said that she changed over a hundred dollars and got ninety-two dollars back. There was a time when the U.S. dollar was the most powerful money in the world. It is no coincidence that the United States is deteriorating.

The United States went from a triple-A credit rating to double-A. Countless of people are without jobs. Many people are losing their houses. The stock market is very shaky. Kingdom is rising against kingdom in the United States. We have a black president. Bible knowledge is on the increase. Christian values are on the decrease. Our nation has moved from one nation under God to one nation under fraud. The Quartet has given Israel and Palestine a mandate to sign the peace treaty by December 2012. Israel has already started sacrificing animals.

Israel is anticipating signing the peace treaty so they can move the sacrifices to the Temple Mount. They consider the Temple Mount the sacred place for the sacrifices. The third temple will start construction once the peace treaty is signed. I wrote about the article I read stating that the temple may not be built, but Israel may just use the Temple Mount. Seeing all these things gives me the authority to say that there has been a shift. Also, the Bible tells us that the wealth of the wicked is laid up for the just. This transfer is taking place at this time. We have to exercise kingdom principles to receive the transfer. I never thought I would be a farmer.

The area where I grew up had no farms. After I moved to North Carolina, I met people who had farms. When I was invited for dinner, we ate vegetables recently pulled out of the garden. After experiencing that, I began wishing that I had learned to farm. I don't have that expertise, but I do have the expertise for kingdom farming. I once worked at a gospel radio station. A preacher came on the air during my time. For thirty minutes Monday through Friday, he would teach. He told me that a lot of the older people in the community would tune in to listen to him. He started teaching seed-planting. He told me that a lot of them stopped listening.

The station had a gospel and R&B format. The owner of the station told me that he had to have the R&B format because the church alone was not enough to support the station, which was a new station. I did the gospel hours while others did the R&B. I started planting seeds in the ministry of the pastor who was doing the faith-seed teaching. I planted seeds toward getting more gospel hours on the station. The pastor would come to the station in the morning to do his teaching. He decided to start doing his Sunday morning service on the air. The engineer at the station had to go to his church and install a remote unit in the church.

The pastor, engineer, and I were at the church at the time. Three people had invested in the radio station, the engineer being one of them. As he was installing the equipment, he stated that they were getting ready to extend the gospel hours on the station. After he said that, I broke out into laughter. He asked what I was laughing about. The pastor responded to him but didn't tell him why I was laughing. Both the pastor and I knew what was going on. It was a result of the seeds I had planted. Eventually the station went completely to gospel. That is what seed-planting will do for you.

This is how the saints of God have to receive their benefits during this hour. That incident took place over twenty years ago. I have been doing the same thing since that time. I planted a seven-hundred-dollar seed into a ministry and very shortly received an unexpected thirty-five-thousand dollar harvest.

While the transfer is taking place, we must seed to tap into it. The Bible says to acknowledge God in all of our ways, and He will direct our path. We must acknowledge God as to people or places we must plant our seed. The Bible also says that we must plant in good ground. Good ground is those ministries that are in the will of God. In this tough economical time, there are people who are using every trick in the book to get a dollar.

I recall some years ago, a preacher came to visit my wife and me. We were discussing the Bible. I mentioned how the devil could give you things. She retorted, saying, "I have a problem with that." She didn't think the devil could offer us anything. What is considered to be the temptations of Jesus, where the devil offered Jesus the kingdoms of the world if he would bow down and worship him, is the model I use to say the devil can offer us stuff. I made that statement to introduce this question: Why is it that so many evil people are monetarily rich? I have a feeling that someone may have been wondering about that after reading this section. I will not attempt to offer an exhausted explanation.

I offer what I consider the main reason. Jesus gave the church a mandate to preach the kingdom throughout the entire world. There are people who say Christians should not be concerned with money because Jesus was poor. There is a scripture stating that Jesus says the birds of the air have nest, the foxes have holes, but the son of man has no place to lay His head. There were people who desired to go along with Jesus and His disciples as they went to different towns to preach the message of the kingdom. Jesus was telling them that on that journey would be an absence of the amenities they were accustomed to at home.

There is another scripture that we must look at. Some of Jesus's disciples asked Him to show them where He lived, and Jesus told them to follow Him and that He would show them where He lived. I can't see myself being a carpenter and not having anywhere to live, can you? When Jesus went on His journeys to spread the gospel of the kingdom, He took His treasurer with Him. Remember Judas? Judas was the treasurer for Jesus and His followers. It came to the light that Judas was a thief. Judas held that position for three years, and prior to Judas receiving thirty pieces of silver to betray Jesus, nowhere in scripture is it suggested that Judas was fired for stealing from the treasure. Jesus had so much money He was not concerned about it.

If that's not convincing enough, why would anybody need a treasurer if he or she were broke? The point is this: it takes money to preach the gospel. The devil is smart enough to know this. The devil's job has been to keep the money out of the hands of the righteous, and in the hands of those who would not be concerned about fulfilling the great commission. Jesus said to preach the gospel to the ends of the earth. A person living in America would find it difficult going to Israel without doing so by airplane. Even an air balloon would cost money. The airlines for some reason or another will not allow an evangelist who's going overseas to preach the gospel to fly for free. I can see it now:

> Hello, sir, my name is Dr. Patterson. I have to fly to India to fulfill my portion of preaching the gospel throughout the entire world. I don't have any money, but if you will give me a roundtrip ticket and feed me on the way there and on the way back, God will bless you. Oh, and by the way, sir, I will need money while I'm in India because I will need somewhere to live while I'm there. Also, I will need to eat. Will you be so kind, sir, as to give me the money I will need while on this mission?

That may be the way things happen for you, but for the other millions of people who've traveled that route, they had to have money. The devil is doing all he can to keep money out of the hands of us who will do

God's will. The mindset that a Christian must be poor to remain humble is straight from the pit of hell.

The problems we are seeing in the world today are threefold. God has to put the money in the hands of His servants to bring His word to fulfillment. It is time to birth the earth into a new a dimension, and we are feeling those labor pains. We need to show humankind that we are not capable of living life free of God's leadership. As I mentioned earlier, we are in the beginning half of the tribulation period. People are still waiting to be snatched away. God is doing what He said He would do. He said that He would keep us out of the tribulation. God is now putting the money in the hands of His people. That is why Wall Street now looks like Main Street.

That is why the housing market went belly up. That is why the government had to bail out the banks and the automobile industry. These things are not mere coincidences. It is no coincidence we have a black president. I have seen God make two miraculous moves to put money into my hands. I am being a blessing whenever I can. I shared in one of my previous books how the enemy had used the people in the local DSS along with the Division of Child Development to close my family's business down. I also stated how the Veterans Administration robbed of my benefits. God made the Veterans Administration pay me back and made them give me the benefits I'm supposed to have.

He also made a way to get the family business opened up again. I said in the previous book that I had started to wait until the storm was over before I completed the book. The Holy Spirit reminded me that we don't wait to shout when the victory is won, we shout as if the victory had already been won. That is why I went on with the book. Now I am able to give my victory report. But God did it, God did it, God did it!

CHAPTER

Why the Prosperity Message?

Many people believed that being poor was a way of showing one's self as being humble. I think those people got humility and stupidity mixed up. The Bible clearly states that if a father wants to give his children good gifts, how much more does your heavenly father want to give good gifts? If you are a parent, and you have no desire to give your children good gifts, just know that your attitude is not the attitude of God. God wants His people to have the desires of their hearts. It is not a sin to desire to have a beautiful house. It is not a sin to desire to have nice things.

The Bible description of heaven lets us know that: the streets are paved with gold. There are pearls and emeralds all about. In answer to the disciples request to teach, then to pray, Jesus tells them to pray in this manner: say, "Our father, who art in heaven hollowed be thy name. Thy kingdom come and thy will be done on earth as it is in heaven." Jesus would not have told them to ask that God's will be done on earth as it is in heaven if that were impossible. It took only God only to speak those into existence.

I have never heard of a person standing at the entrance of a train and saying to the conductor, "In the name of Jesus, I stand here in California, and I command a ticket to be in your hand that will allow me to ride to New York." Someone may know something different from what I know, but I think the conductor will want to see a ticket that was purchased by you. The prosperity message comes from people being ignorant of what God wants us to have. Too many of God's people are living below their covenant entitlement. It is the plan of Satan to attack the message.

.Many attacks on the prosperity message come because Satan knows of the damage it would do to his kingdom. There are those who label preacher as prosperity preachers. All preachers should be prosperity preachers. In 3 John 3:2, it says, "Beloved, I wish above all things that you prosper and be in health even as your soul prospers." I believe that some people attack the message because of their inability to generate income. A person who calls him or herself a Christian is supposed to apply the keys of the kingdom so that God can supply his or her needs. The keys of the kingdom are the same as saying the principles of the kingdom. That is why God told us to seek first His kingdom.

Jesus tells us to not be concerned about what we will eat, what we will wear, what we will drive, or where we would live, but to seek or make the kingdom your priority. When we make the kingdom our priority, we will find ourselves in a position to concentrate on giving instead of all the time trying to get. People have their priorities out of order. Many people place too much attention on asking God for things He said that comes automatically. He tells us to seek the kingdom and all these will be added. Preachers have to preach the prosperity message to get people to understand the kingdom.

We must realize that we are ambassadors in a foreign country. The ambassadors are backed by their countries, just as U.S. ambassadors in other countries are backed by the Unites States. An ambassador has diplomatic immunity. An ambassador from another country that is placed in the United States will claim diplomatic immunity in a New York minute. Kingdom of God people must understand that as ambassadors from heaven, we have diplomatic immunity. When poverty attempts to rob us of our right to abundance, we must claim diplomatic immunity. The people who fight the prosperity message are people who do not know who they are. They are people who do not realize that the job they are on is not their source. They are there to influence the lost.

When people do not know who they are, there is certainty that they do not know the authority they have in the earth. God placed Adam on the earth to dominate it. Adam gave it away. Many people are doing the same thing. We are here to dominate. Too many of us are being dominated. God tells Abraham that He will bless those who bless him and curse those who curse him. The Bible also tells us that if we are in Christ, we are Abraham's seed. We have an inheritance from Father Abraham. The same rule applies to God's ambassadors. There are people out there who are supposed to be blessing us. They have to bless us whether they want to or not. There are people of influence who do things for people and can't understand why.

Anything that is legal to have, and people fight against having it, is a sure way to know the influence comes from the depths of hell. The devil's job is to keep God's people blinded to the kingdom pleasures we are privileged to have. The richest man that ever lived made this statement; money answers all things. If Israel would pay Palestine enough money, that government would be glad to give up the land that Israel already own. There would not be those tensions toward each other. The right amount of money would cause Iran to leave Israel alone. The right amount of money would cause righteous women to become unrighteousness. Don't get upset, ladies; the same thing applies to us guys.

One of the main causes for divorce is finances. A woman would stay in a lousy marriage if the money is right. Of course, that does not apply to all women, just the ones I know. The richest man that ever lived is, of course, King Solomon. Anyone with seven hundred wives and three hundred girlfriends definitely gets my attention. I am doing all I can to please one wife. It's taking everything I've got to do that. There were times when I had to borrow a few things to keep my reputation intact. I can't wait to see that brother. I've got a whole lot of questions for him. It takes money to influence the people we are supposed to influence in the earth. Someone who is broke doesn't influence me at all.

I think it is time to bring you back to my title. It all has to do with one's children being out of control. Many of us have children we have to deal with. As I said in the beginning, we have to deal with those issues we have carried with us since childhood. A lot of those issues are not realized until we enter into certain relationships. It is my opinion that a marital relationship brings out every issue we have. There are casual relationships that don't carry the expectations a marital relationship carry. It is because of the high expectations of the marital relationship we find those issues exposed.

I recall many years ago, I had run into one of my friends. We were talking when a young lady walked by. I expressed my evaluation of the young lady. He was aware that I had a girlfriend. He said, "What about your girlfriend?" My response to him was that I was not married. I didn't require the values of a marriage, nor did I feel required to give them. That is one of the reasons I say the issues we carry into a marriage are not realized in other relationships. If I had a control issue, that issue would not have been realized in that relationship. There are so many issues that we acquired during childhood. I like to use the five painful areas as a means of recognizing our issues. As a reminder, those areas are molestation, incest, rejection, physical abuse, and emotional abuse.

In my counseling manual, I list the ramifications of each one. I use them as a gauge to show people what direction they need to take to bring forth change in their life. I label those areas as painful because they produce pain in our lives. I talk about three types of people. The oppressed, the suppressed, and the repressed people are the ones I deal with. I will give an example of the repressed people. They are unaware that anything has affected them that would cause problems in their adult life. They have blocked the memory because of the intense trauma he or she experienced. This person will exhibit periods of depression and have thoughts of suicide.

Some of these people may experience inexplicable physical pain. I believe that all of the painful areas lead to these painful ramifications: loss of self-respect, fear of knowledge, fear of rejection, anger, and bitterness. I bump these five basic areas against the types of people. I then determine a course of action. I entered marriage with many issues. It took seven years to learn about the problems I had. It took several years to get healed from them. I wanted to be a theologian. The Bible college I attended for bachelor's degree dealt with theology and counseling. Counseling was the last thing I wanted to get involved with. I couldn't stand counseling. I began to prepare myself for the graduate program.

Prior to starting school, God told me to go into counseling. I did not want to, but I knew I had to be obedient. I ended up falling in love with counseling. I ended up getting a doctorate in theology, but it was after I received my counseling credentials. It got to the point where I could not stand theology. I reached a conclusion concerning theology. My definition of theology is man's way of making a simple gospel difficult. We have come into a new season. In this season, it is imperative that we deal with those inner children. Those inner children make it impossible to believe God on the level we need to believe Him.

In 3 John 3:2, the matter concerning the inner children is made clear. We must review the soul's different compartments to see the clearness of the matter. The compartments we will explore are the mind, will, emotions, intellect, and imagination. I always have to revert to this truth to justify why I say what I say. I believe the emotions are to the soul what the immune system is to the body because it is so important to our perception of life to feel about ourselves the way God would have us to feel. God wants us to believe about ourselves the things He says about us. God says that we are a royal priesthood. A person who has low self-esteem has it because he or she does not believe what God said. We have to believe what God says about us.

In the study of child development, there are those who advocate the cognitive development of a child standing out as the preponderance to development. On the other hand, there are those who advocate the affective construct as holding the preponderance. The affective construct is the emotional side of development, while the cognitive construct is the intellectual side of development. I am aware of many educated people who have a low self-esteem. On the other hand, I am aware of uneducated people who have a high self-esteem. Also, I am aware of uneducated people who are far more successful than are educated people. In my estimation, that equates to the emotional side of development as carrying the most weight.

I recall back when I was seventeen years old I was working with a fellow who was training me in carpentry. He was not only a carpenter; he was also a womanizer. He would point out the woman he was going after; then he would bring pictures of him and her in the mix. He made this statement to me: "Man, if you tell those women how good they look, you can get just about get anything you want." In essence, he was saying that if a man makes a woman feel good about herself, she was prey. However, some, he told me, were hard cases. My assessment of this situation is that the women he was able to conquer were the women who had a low view of themselves. He was able to make them feel good about themselves to the point they wanted to reward him. Furthermore, the ones he was unable to conquer were the women who already felt good about themselves and did not need an added push.

This is why I came up with the notion that the emotions are to the soul what the immune system is to the body. When people feel good about themselves, like a jet breaking the sound barrier, we break the sound barrier with our ideas. When people feel bad about themselves, it affects the other components in a negative way. They don't feel like they can learn. It is difficult for them to imagine themselves as being successful. They think they are unable to succeed.

That is why it is especially important to deal with those inner children in this season. Very shortly, we are going to have to depend on God like never before. A people who do not believe that they are what God says we are, are certainly not going to believe what He says we can do. We can no longer depend on the government. We must understand kingdom aspects to be successful in this season. I find it really amazing how politicians are really dogging each other concerning the way the country should be run. They just don't get it. Our country has changed forever. As I wrote earlier concerning the season we are in, things are the way they are according to Biblical prophecy.

Evangelicals who believe in the pre-rapture theory are ignorant as to the season we are in. They are waiting to be raptured up so the tribulation can began. As far as I know, I am the only one who's saying that the tribulation has already begun. There are those who believe in the post-rapture, but they think the tribulation is only three and a half years, so they don't exactly know what time it is either. When God spoke to me in 2005 and told me about times of the black man, I could not find anyone else who He had spoken to about it. It took two years before I got a confirmation. It did not come from a black person; it came from a white person. The people I told about it did not believe me. It seems that I am in that predicament again.

Back in 2006, when I told people we were getting ready for a black president, only one person believed me. Although she believed me, she also thought it would be in another twenty years. This time, I am not feeling the way I did about that situation. I am more secure in my belief. I have shared my position with people who didn't say they disagreed, but they said that it could be possible. I don't see why others don't see it. The banks, the housing industry, the automobile industry, Wall Street, the bad global economy, and high unemployment—why would anyone consider this to be coincidence?

The writing is on the wall. I keep giving hints to the class I teach at True Apostolic School of Theology. I can't teach it as a full discipline because it doesn't line up with the coursework. Watching what is happening with the money that rich carnal people have is very interesting. There are several different classes when it comes to rich people. There are the saved rich people, who are carnal in their spending, and there are the wicked rich people, who are carnal in their actions. The rich people who are saved but carnal will see their dollars fly away as well as the evil rich people. It is also interesting to see how many people will take the mark of the beast as a means to maintain their riches.

At the end of 2008, when how bad the economy was became clear, a scripture in the book of Revelations kept ringing in my ears. I kept hearing: "Babylon has fallen, has fallen." Along with the signs, I mentioned earlier, I must add that scripture tells us about a time when we won't be able to tell the seasons apart. As I write this section of the book, it is February 2012. It feels summer in an area where it is normally too cold to blow your nose outside. There are so many signs that suggest we are in the time spoken of by the prophet Daniel, from whom we get our seventieth week. We are in the beginning of sorrows. With this being the beginning, we may want to tighten our seatbelts because we are about to take a ride that will make any ride at Six Flags seem like a Sunday picnic.

Spiritual rich people, and that's Spiritual with a capital S, which refers to those who do the godly things with their money. There are people who will be setting the example for the wicked. Not only will an example be set for spending, but it will also serve as a catalyst to the realness of God. God's principles of the kingdom as it pertains to money will become a reality to the unbeliever. I know we are moving toward a cashless society, but we who are leaning on God's kingdom will be successful regardless of the system we would have to use.

The bible teachers who taught that the church would be snatched up have really hurt the church. By teaching that the church would not be here during tribulation, there has been no teaching on what to expect or what to do during this time. There have been so many years wasted with arguing back and forth on the pre-rapture, the mid-rapture, and the post-rapture theories. I went along with the pre-rapture theory because I did not understand the book of Revelations. It was more appealing for me to not have to be concerned about such stormy events. I think many people took lightly what Daniel says in his prophecies. God tells Daniel that the prophecies of that book are sealed until times of the end. The teachings that are out before the times of the end are erroneous.

CHAPTER

Dairy of an Angry Black Man

I can't help but think that the generation before mine, which is the Depression generation, was a generation of people marked by anger. This concept applies to black people. I'm sure the generations of black people were angry too, but I have to reference this generation because this is the generation my father comes from. In 1973, I entered the military. I was surrounded by very discriminative white people. I could hardly believe it. I didn't understand why people would treat people that way knowing that they would have to depend on these people for their very life. It caused me to question as I stated before.

I figured that if I were having the experience I was having, what was it like for my father in World War II? While I was stationed at Fort Bragg, North

Carolina, during one of my weekend visits with my parents, I asked my father about his experience in the military. He informed me of the black–white army. He told me that the black soldiers fought separately from the white soldiers. He stated that there were black captains and lieutenants, but they could only give orders to the black soldiers. He stated that the only time they were together was in the mess hall. He then replied with a very angry inflection that he would never forget what one of the white soldiers said to him: "I don't see why we have to eat in here with these niggers."

I didn't understand the dangers of pass hurts at the time, but after I got involved with counseling, I thought back to that time and realized where some of his anger had originated. As I stated elsewhere, I had a friend in my unit at the time who was white. We had become very close. I had a four-hour drive from Fort Bragg to home, so I could visit my family fairly often. On one occasion, I asked my friend to come along with me. He agreed, and we drove home that weekend. My friends liked him, and we all had a nice time that weekend. Approximately three years later, I received some input from my mother. She told me that my father did not like the idea of me bringing my friend to his house. I don't know what took her so long to tell me. My father's military experience along with what was taking place in our society had produced one angry black man.

I'm sure there were countless angry black men who had similar experiences in our society. I am a baby boomer, and I had a bad experience with racial discrimination. I hate to think about what they went through. It is 2012, and I am still experiencing a great deal of racial discrimination. In the town I now live in, it makes me feel like I'm living in the sixties and seventies. I now live in Sanford, North Carolina, where my wife is from.

My wife has told me about times when the Klu Klux Klan would gather on a certain road in Sanford. Not being from this town, I wasn't familiar with the people who were involved in these meetings. I found out some time later about some of those who were active members. My wife and I wanted to start a day-care business in this same town. There was only one black day-care center at the time. The center had at one time been owned by white occupants. There were fewer tactics to be used by the white officials who hate to see black people advance in this city. The standards for day-care facilities were already established because of the prior owners, so the person didn't have many obstacles before starting. My wife and I, on the other hand, had to jump through hoops to get our business started.

Those prejudiced city officials did everything they could to prevent us from opening. I had to be persistent, or we would have never started our business. After we were opened, we continued to come up against racial resistance. I started complaining about racial discrimination. I fought back but did not fight the way God would have wanted me to. I did it my way. As a result, I found myself getting in trouble. God was there for me, although I had stepped outside of His will. I learned a valuable lesson from that experience. The people involved in the evil practices retorted with this: "He is only saying that because of the situation he got himself in."

It is a shame the way government entities do not have to be liable for their wrongs. I spoke to an attorney about the wrong and evil things the government workers did, and he told me that they had sovereign immunity. They may have it with humans but not with God. One by one, the evil people started leaving the positions they held. Some years later, the head of the group I'm referring to did something that exposed the truth I had brought out some ten years back. To her subordinates, she sent an e-mail of a man hanging from a noose. A black worker at the facility got hold of it and reported it to the news channel in Raleigh. It made the news and was on the Internet.

To my understanding, there were a couple of meetings held by the city officials of her peers who determined that it did not merit her being relieved of her position. I knew it would turn out that way. I spoke to the person who represents the National Association for the Advancement of Colored People (NAACP) for Sanford, and he told me that the

NAACP was still investigating. He asked me if I would be available to give my input concerning this person. There are a lot of things I could say of this nature concerning my experience in this town, but I will have to wait and write those things in my new book, which will be titled *Sanford, 1950 in 2012*.

The experience I have had in this town alone could have produced much anger. I'm glad that I have learned to practice the presence of God. By continuing to praise God through it all, I was able to maintain my joy. The Bible tells us that the joy of the Lord is our strength. In the presence of God, there is joy. However, I was not always aware of the praise principle. As a matter of fact, I wasn't walking with God during the years anger was produced in my life. I would have to say that it started with my father. Judging by what my father told me about his military experience along with his postmilitary experience, I would conclude that he was very angry.

I have to reiterate what I wrote in a previous book concerning my childhood experience. My father was a good man. He took good care of his family and set a good example for me in terms of how women should be treated. However, I feel that he carried anger from his past. Because of that anger, he was impetuous. I was the first born among the boys in the family. I was the one he practiced on. He was very physical with me. I got more whippings than I can count. I was both emotional and physically abused.

When we look at the five painful areas I spoke of earlier, I find myself being affected by three of them. There are some basic ramifications that are conducive to all who affected by them. There are five basic effects I deal with. There is the loss of self-respect, fear of knowledge, fear of rejection, anger, and bitterness. I say basic because each individual will have these effects in different degrees. What affects me in a grave manner may affect another person only on the surface. There are the effects that psychologists come up with, but psychology treads on dangerous ground. What is demonic is explained through psychology as being some type of inappropriate behavior pattern. Psychology has to be careful as to not give any credence to the spiritual because it would put a lot of professionals out of work.

This is why I stick to my five basic ramifications. In doing so, I am able to gauge where the problem came from and how to chart a course that would bring forth change. That is why I was able to rid myself of the anger produced in me by my father. My father sowed anger in me. I reaped fury. The Bible makes it clear that the harvest always overshadows the seed. The anger I operated with was produced by my father. I was so uncomfortable around my father. I tried in every way I could find to avoid his presence. I tried if at all possible not to initiate a conversation with him. I could stir up some anger in him if I did not give him the proper response. He would backhand me in a New York minute.

I found myself responding to people in authority the same way I responded to father. I was very uncomfortable around authority. Even after I found myself in a position of authority, I still avoided as much as possible those who were in authority over me. There was a time when I felt that people in positions of authority were the enemy. I watched *Praise the Lord* on TBN one night when Bishop T. D. Jakes interviewed one of his daughters. She referenced being able to come together as a group and talk about those things that affected us in childhood and that are being masked. We will look at the awesome way in which God uses Bishop Jakes.

The truth of the matter is that rather you're a bishop, an archbishop, a pope, or something else, you're still a human being. There are no perfect fathers outside of our heavenly father. I don't have the authority to say that there is not a person on the earth who was not affected in a negative way at least to some degree during their childhood, but I do have the authority to say that no one's perfect. I believe there are some sons who were affected in a negative way by their fathers, but pale in comparison to the way I was affected. A father can affect a child in several ways. He can affect his children by not being in the home. He can also affect his children by being there and exercising improper disciplinary methods.

I recall wishing that my father would find himself a place to live other than with me. When I began training for the ministry, I was at a revival at the church of the pastor who was training me. He invited a prophet to come in and run the revival. On the first night of the revival, after he had finished speaking, he called a prayer line. I was hesitant about going up for prayer. He waited until finally I decided to go up. When I got up there he stated that he was waiting for me to come up because he didn't like having to call people up. When I got up there, I realized that he was God's servant, and that he represented God at that moment. In my mind, I was standing in the presence of God.

I started getting that uneasy feeling that I would get when I was around my father. I was so messed up that I was scared to death. If you were to speak to the guys in my neighborhood during my twenties, they would choke to hear me say that I was scared to death. I was so rugged at that time that I would have fought Muhammad Ali without having to get in shape. Anyway, I learned then that the way a father handles a child is the way that child is going to feel about God. That incident took place approximately twenty-five years ago. I would always tell people that they saw God the way they saw their father. I never heard anyone else say it. When we are out on a limb, we have the propensity to keep it quiet.

I kept saying it anyway. Finally, this year, 2012, I was looking at the It's Supernatural website by Sid Roth, and he had a guest on his program who said the same thing. I can't recall her name. I finally got a confirmation after twenty years. While I can speak of the negative side of my father, I also have to speak of the positive side. Being a father myself, I'm sure my children would have some negative things to say about me. I wouldn't want them to just bring out the negative things. I would also like to hear some positive things.

My father was very responsible when it came to his family. He made sure we had everything we needed. I recall one of my sisters saying that my father would tell everyone to make a list at Christmas time. She stated that he would tell us that he may not be able to get everything on the list, but he would try to. She concluded with him getting us everything on our list each year. He taught us to be respectful. He made sure we went to church. I recall us sitting down to the supper table together every day. I believe his leadership caused us to become a tightly knitted family. I never heard him or my mother curse. Surely my children don't have that testimony. Although his issues brought on my issues, I still have reason to be proud of my father. I can plainly understand the issues he had and why he had them. It was difficult for parents of the Depression generation.

They experienced a degree of racial discrimination that the baby-boomer generation did not experience. Anyway, after my father's death, my mother made the statement to me that my father was a good man. The wife of a man will make the best judgment of her husband's character. I have to applaud my father for not teaching his children to be partial toward white people. I can't recall any adult of the Depression generation that I came in contact with giving any regard to being partial toward white people. That was a special generation. I know there were some who attempted to retaliate, but I didn't know them.

Coupled with my father's influence was that of a few of my sisters. One of my sisters went along with the other in producing a lot of negativity in my life. I was told by one of my sisters that I was very ugly and that I would never be able to get a girlfriend. She suggested that I not smile because smiling only added to the "ug" on my mug. I know that they had no idea how the things they did and said would affect me. The problem with that is that ignorance does not prevent principles from working. When people feed negativity into a child who has no idea of who he or she is, the child has the propensity to believe the things he or she has been told. They frequently criticized things I did or said.

The influence they had on me during that time produced a lot of wrong ideas I had about myself. It carried a lot of weight during my school years. I was afraid to give my opinion in class. I felt that my opinion would be stupid and that I would be laughed at. I was very quiet in school. I didn't think I could accomplish anything. I didn't try very hard because of such thinking. I felt that everyone were better than I was. I was very good in football and basketball, but I didn't think I was good enough to compete with others. I stood out in the community when it came to sports, but in the back of mind, I thought that I would be a failure in school competition. It took the military for my thinking to change.

I have one sister who took a special interest in me. She assisted me in learning. I don't know why she took such an interest in me, and even after all of these years, I have never asked her why. I think I am going to take the time out to call her and ask her why. I may not like the answer she gives me, which may be the reason I was never concerned about asking her. She has been there for me even until this day. My other sisters call her my favorite sister. I never told anyone that. My wife calls her my second mother.

I recall her helping me to learn to write my name. When I would spell my name, I would make a capitol *E* and instead of putting one line in the middle, I would put three or four. That may have something to do with why she took such an interest in me. I had a lot to overcome once I entered adulthood. It took quite a few years before I realized I had something to overcome. A lot of my thinking changed after I entered the military, and I thought I was all right. It was ten years later when I realized that I had some real issues to deal with. It was at that time when I realized how my childhood had been affected. When I consider the influences that caused me to be an angry black man, I must say a few things about my elementary school experience. I had transferred from an all-black elementary school to an elementary school that had just begun desegregation.

This school had an influence that I never can forget. The principal admitted that he was prejudiced. He also stated that he was working at overcoming his prejudices. I believe there are a lot of white people who were taught to be prejudicial. I know of one person this happened to. I had two friends who were married. The husband was black, and the wife was white. The wife had a friend who would come over and visit. I told the wife that I was interested in talking to her friend. She communicated my desire to her friend. The next time I saw her friend she told me that her parents told her to never get involved with a black man. I thought that to be ridiculous. I want say that she was an ugly girl, but I will say that she wasn't all of that either. It didn't break my heart to hear it. But this is how I know that there were white parents who taught their children to be partial toward black people.

The black children at that school had to jump through hoops to get where we needed to get. There was so much favoritism shown to the white kids. The school as a whole was a bad influence on the black kids. There were some white teachers who seemed to have adjusted well. My sixth-grade teacher said something that was really remarkable. She stated that black people could move better than white people when we danced.

I didn't know how valuable that statement was at the time. I started out in the band in the fifth grade. I was kicked out of the band by a white band teacher who appeared to me to be very racist. By the time I was in the sixth grade, the school had a new band teacher. I got back in the band. I wanted to play the trombone, but he made me play the baritone. I didn't like that move, but at least I was in the band. The band at that time was predominately black. The school would put on a concert at the end of each school year. The school would have children come from another school to assist with the concert. By the time I was in the seventh grade, the band teacher told the principal that we did not need assistance from the other school.

We handled our business. It was amazing how we were able to do the concert that year without any assistance. There were some black guys I grew up with who also attended the school. They would not put up with the way black children were being treated. I recall one of my friends challenging the principal to a dual. I didn't think much of it at the time, but as I look back, I find it amazing how a child in elementary school challenged a principal to a fight. In my mind, I had to go along with the way things were because, after all, we black people were inferior to white people; that was the way things were supposed to be. I suspect that I had a slave mentality.

Some of the issues that were born out of the way I was affected at home showed up once I reached junior high school. Junior high is no longer used now. The term used now is middle school. Also, the system has changed from the way it was when I was in elementary school. I went to the seventh grade while in elementary school. Now the seventh grade starts in middle school. I was in the eighth grade when I arrived at middle school. I started in the summer session. I had continued in the band because we had to practice over the summer to be prepared when school started. I felt that I did not have what the other students had. In my mind, I was below all the other students.

I was of the mind-set that I could not accomplish what the other students could accomplish. I was very quiet in class. I did not want to be embarrassed by my silly opinion of anything. I had become interested in girls at that time, but I was too shy to try to talk to any of them. I felt that I could never give them anything they would be interested in. I didn't realize what was going on. For instance, the majority of the people in my classes were from the projects. I didn't know what it meant to live in the projects at that time. I lived in a suburb and had no clue how they viewed me. I learned much later what was really going on. After I went to the ninth grade, I began to get an idea of what I had going on.

I found out that some girls were interested in me. I couldn't understand why. After all, I had been told by my sister that I would never be able to get a girlfriend. One girl had relatives across the street from where I lived. When she would come to visit them, she would always seek me out. I was always nervous around her because of what I believed about myself. Other girls in my classes showed interest in me, but I was too afraid to follow up on the notion. It was probably good for me that things turned out the way they did. If I would have sought those girls, my life would probably be a mess. I probably would have about twenty children.

My greatest accomplishments in middle school happened in the band room. I was in the ninth grade and was first chair in my section. The yearly festival was coming up, and we were preparing for it. By being first chair, I had to play all of the solos. Our band director had informed the band that the judges listening to us at the festival were prejudice and would never give us the recognition we deserved. I knew that my work was cut out for me. I had to play in a manner as to make those judges change their minds about the way they rated us.

Our band director told us that every year our school entered the festival, the judges would give our school a three or four regardless of how we sounded. He said that they never would give us a "one" even if we deserved it. He said that there was a black man who fought to have a black person as one of the judges. He also stated that the man had to back off because he nearly lost his job. That's the way it was for black people at that time. Our band director wanted to really impress those judges this time. He got another band director from another school to assist him as we practiced for the festival. We practiced during the band hour at school, and then we met after school and practiced late into the evening. My father told me to get a note from the band director to indicate that I was spending my time at the school. My father thought that I was trying to pull one over on him. I got the note from the band director, and my father was all right with it then.

During our practicing, the guest band director would have me play my solo. I liked using vibrato when I played. The guest director thought I was nervous. He told me to not be nervous when I play. I didn't bother to explain; I just played it the way he wanted me to. After months of practice the time came to perform. If I didn't know any better, I would say that the night was magical. We sounded so good that night. I played my solos with precision.

The following Monday when we got back to school, the band director had written something on the board: "They gave us a two, but I know we deserved a one. I am proud of all of you. You all can be proud too." I know we deserved a one. They robbed us that night. That was the way it was and the influence I had at that time. After middle school, I went on to high school at Booker T. Washington, which had the best high school band in the country. We were a group of talented young people. We played all the latest hits that were out. During a parade, all the people would follow our band. Our band director, Mr. Walker, was a musical genius.

I had an exciting time in high school. In 1971, it was ordered by the state to start desegregation. High school kids from predominately white schools had to be bused to our school and vice versa. I was fortunate enough to have been going into the twelfth grade at the time. Those who would be seniors the following year were not bused. After the order was given, the city came in and painted the school. We got brand-new books, and they even painted the lockers in the school. A few years later, they tore down the old school and built a new one. The school was very old. It did not matter to the city until their children had to come there. That was the way we lived at that time.

It was such a struggle for black people. It is still a struggle but much different than it was back then. Black people always had to fight for what we wanted. I became a little more active in high school. I was still shy and timid, but I wasn't as deep in the shell as I had been in middle school. My head was right at the exit. I even got a girlfriend at that time. I joined an R&B singing group while in high school. We were all members of the high school band. We would travel to different places and perform concerts. It was at that time, I decided to try my hand at drinking. It did not work for me.

I recall doing a show at the Virginia Beach Dome, and we had a party afterward. I had never seen so much booze in one place. I started drinking as if I had been doing it all along. I had on an all-white outfit that night, and when I woke up at home the next day wondering how I got there, my outfit was red. I don't know why I was throwing up blood. The band members who had brought me home told me that they had to put me in the trailer with the instruments. About a year after high school, the majority of the members ended up going to New Jersey and became a national recording R&B group. A few of the guys went on to college. I went into the military.

Although I had some fun times, I was still influenced by the ill treatment of our divided society. It did not get any better in the military. I saw a great deal of discrimination in the military. I couldn't understand how some of the soldiers would show themselves as being racist because it was so easy to deal with them in a combat situation. If a few black soldiers went on a recon with a white soldier who was known to be a racist, they could cause an accident to take place that would cause that soldier to have a bad day. I guess when it's deeply rooted it is hard to come out of it. When I was in the 82nd Airborne Division, we would be on different cycles during the year. One of the cycles was division ready force, or DRF. We had DRF 1, 2, and 3.

If we were on DRF 3, we could leave the post but had to be able to be contacted in the event of an alert. We did not have cell phones then, so we had to be at a house where we could be reached by phone. I had a buddy who lived in Winston-Salem, and we went to his house while we were on DRF 3. He took me to a house where booze was sold. We had to call in to give our unit the number to where we were. We did not get called out that night. The very next day, which was Saturday, we got called on alert. We all rushed as we got in our uniforms and on the road back to Fort Bragg.

I was driving, and I drove like a mad man. I did not want to be late getting back. Good thing we did not get called that night. We were the last ones to get back. As soon as we checked in, the first sergeant reported that everyone was present and accounted for. As soon as that was done, we were back on the road back to Winston-Salem. That was one of the fun times I had in the military.

I had a lot of not-so-fun times. On one occasion, we were on DRF 1, and everyone had to stay in the barracks. The married guys who lived off-post still had to occupy a space in the barracks. We were all in the barracks, and there was disturbance in the hallway just outside our room. There were three of us in the room, and the other two guys were white. One asked the other about the situation in the hallway, adding, "You know how those niggers are." He thought about what he said and then tried to dress it up. It is difficult to hide what's really inside. I could have started a race riot that day, but I decided to ignore it and act as if I had not heard it. We had a platoon sergeant who was racist. I was up for promotion, and I had to get a recommendation from him to get it. He would not give me the recommendation though. I knew I deserved the promotion. He got orders to go for some special training in Georgia. He was gone for two months.

A black staff sergeant had to take his place in his absence. He gave me the recommendation that I needed, and I got my promotion to sergeant. When the platoon sergeant came back and saw the stripes on my collar, he turned a color that I still cannot describe. That was in 1975. I had quite a few incidents similar to those events. Trying to recall them all would mean that I would have to change the title of the book to *The Military's Anti-black Campaign*. I don't want people to miss the point of what I'm trying to convey—I am writing my diary of the events that caused the angry black man I used to be.

Spelling out those events is quite necessary. It will help facilitate the reader's confidence concerning the principles I talk about in this book that I applied, and that those same principles will help in the lives of others. I had experienced so much racial discrimination in my life that I didn't think the time would come when I would move beyond it. I'm not saying that it has subsided, but I am saying that I have come to a place where I can get around it. I recall back in 2009 when I heard Reverend Al Sharpton give a warning to black people about a black president. He stated that discrimination has in no way been removed from our society and that we must continue to be on our watch. I'm in agreement with that advice.

Although I was so accustomed to racial discrimination, I was blindsided when I went back to college to major in early childhood education. I wasn't aware that women wanted the field exclusively. I was able to experience what women felt when they were not allowed to get into certain fields. First, the instructors took me as a joke. I think they were expecting me to eventually drop the program. I had been going to school approximately one year before they realized that I was in it for the long haul. A student at one point asked the instructor what I was doing there. I really caught it from both students and faculty. I wanted to give up.

I am a resilient person, so I just collected myself and continued on my journey. I was going to school under vocational rehabilitation through the Veterans administration. They decided to give me a little of what I earned. I had to maintain a full-time courseload to get paid for full time. One instructor ticked me off so bad that I told her that I was going to quit. She went to the VA representative and told him that I had quit her class. The VA representative contacted the VA and informed them that I had gone from full-time to three-quarter time. The VA subtracted the money from my monthly pay. I did not actually quit the class; I was just upset at the time. That's what she wanted.

I made an appointment with the president of the college to let him know what the instructor did. I told him in a very nice way that if that ever happened again I would file legal charges. He responded, "I think I know what you're saying, and I will speak to her." The next time I had that class, she asked me to step outside of the classroom. She told me that she really thought I was dropping the class and that was why she did that. She went back into the classroom and would not allow me to respond. It is not the job of an instructor to do that. She had stepped outside of her authority in an attempt to cause me to lose money.

When it came close to graduation time for me, the chairperson told me to settle for just a diploma. I was too close to receiving my degree, so I continued and received my degree. I had it coming at me from all angles. The worse angle was from the city of Sanford. God had His way of getting me to Sanford. It was an arduous method used, but sometimes God has to do things to cause His will to come forth. After I was here a few short months, I asked God why He sent me here. God made it clear to me that He did not send people places that were built up; He sent people to places that need to be built up. I have challenged the system here as it pertains to racial discrimination. I found that there were so many black Sanford natives who lie down and accept the lot that was handed to them.

It would not be so for me. I could not just stand back, watch what was going on, and not say anything. For three years, I worked at an outreach mission operated by the church I attended. I got the opportunity to see discrimination at its worse. We housed the homeless, fed the hungry, clothed the clothes-less, and counseled the misguided. A board formed for the mission to collect donations.

My spiritual mentor told me that it was an all-white board, and that they were really in business for themselves. I could not understand that. It was a struggle to feed, house, and clothe the people we assisted. She told me that the board was receiving money from people in the city, but was not providing it to the mission. I ran the mission at night. People would come in the early hours in the morning because they had nowhere to go and did not have money for a hotel. There were families who came at times. Many of them were only passing through. There were times that I had to reach in my pocket to buy food for them. We did not discriminate. There were more white people being assisted than there were black people. We were assisting those who were fighting against us.

My pastor, Bishop Thomas, told me of some situations that took place during the first year of the mission. He stated that he had received a call from the sheriff office concerning a person who needed assistance. He said the sheriff informed him that the person was white. He told me that he told the sheriff that he didn't care. I deduced that the sheriff made that statement because of the way they treated black people. That was only a drop in the bucket compared to the discrimination I faced in the years to come.

I won't go into a lot of details concerning my racial experiences because they are too numerous to put into this book. I have to say something about the local Division of Social Services (DSS) though. My wife and I opened a child-care facility that assisted parents who received assistance from Social Services. I had a degree in early childhood education, so I met the qualification for being a director. My wife had to go to school for Administration 1 and 2 to qualify for the position. I was the director listed by the state of

North Carolina. I had several black parents come to me and tell me that Social Services told them not to bring their children to our facility. Of course, I did not have any white parents at that time.

After hearing from these parents, I realized why. We were a new facility without a history. There could be no other reason for the people at DSS to tell parents not to support our business except that of racial discrimination. I fought them every step of the way. Of course, they denied it every step of the way.

I wonder what people think of that same supervisor recently caught sending an e-mail to her white employees of a man hanging from a noose. We were in operation for nearly ten years when the DSS found a way to get us closed down. They made up some lies and convinced the Division of Child Development that they were telling the truth. We stayed closed for a few years and opened again.

Prior to our closing, we had to go to court in Raleigh. We had a black judge. The judge was asking questions of our opponents because the things they were saying just did not add up. I'm sure the judge could see the conspiracy. The judge was going up against the attorney general's office. He excused himself from the case. He really should have ruled in our favor. I'm sure he did not want to do that because he would have been risking his job. I'm not like him. It doesn't matter how much opposition I stir up. We either believe God or we don't. I believe God. God made sure that we were well-taken care of during that ordeal.

The state of North Carolina assigned a consultant to each county. These consultants inspect a childcare facility to ensure the facility is in compliance with the state's rules. The consultant for Lee County was someone to reckon with. I complained about her to the region supervisor. I asked her if I could send a petition around to each facility. She did not want to do that. She told me to gather all the directors of the facilities so she could meet with us. I didn't want to do that. I just let the matter go. I later picked the matter back up. I contacted my representative. He put me in touch with a pastor who had a childcare facility in his church. I met with the pastor, and he told me the reason the representative wanted me to contact him.

He stated that he had a problem with this same consultant. He stated that he and the representative were good friends. As a result of the consultant harassing him, he reported the consultant to the representative. He stated that after he did that, the consultant had not been to his facility in several years. The consultant is supposed to inspect at least once a year. After my facility opened back up, the state assigned a different consultant to my facility. I don't know why the state allows the consultant to continue terrorizing the facilities. I sent out surveys to some of the facilities. I received some back with responses from the directors that sounded like they were ready to close down.

The other agency that had given me a lot of problems is the VA. Many people are aware of how the VA mistreats veterans. The VA treats veterans like they were the friends of the people we fought against. They seem to be paying us back for hurting their friends. I have been fighting the VA ever since I left the military in 1986.

CHAPTER

Diary of an Angry
Black Woman

My wife wrote this chapter to tell her story.

I grew up in a very abusive household. My father was a long-distance truck driver. He was away most of the days during the week, but he would be home for the weekends. I would thank God that he was away during the week. I grew up in the country. We lived down a dirt road up in the woods. The dirt road was approximately a mile off of the main highway. There were seven girls and one boy in my family. We would be outdoors playing and could hear my father's truck coming down the dirt road when he was coming in from his road trip. Whenever I would hear that truck coming in, fear would grip my heart.

I would become very nervous because I knew what to expect. He would beat on my mother the way people would beat on stray dogs when they are running them off of their property. It seemed as if it pleased him to beat on her. I can remember those days and events as if they were taking place today. My mother was a beautiful woman. She had long, pretty hair that ran down her back. He would take her by her hair and pull it for no reason at all. He would say very negative things to her and about her. I believe he was jealous of her relationship with her children. We would have so much fun with our mother. She would get out in the yard and play with us as if she were still a child herself.

I think there were times when she did not see us as her children, but as the friends she never had. My mother was not allowed to have friends unless my father approved of them. I recall a family gathering we had with our family on our father side of the family. Everybody was dancing, laughing, and having a wonderful time. My daddy's brothers liked dancing with my mother because she was an excellent dancer. My daddy decided to leave the gathering and go back to our house. He told my mother that he would see us when we get back to the house. My mother said OK, and we stayed there a while longer as we continued to have fun. My daddy was at the house when we got there.

He was sitting in the dark smoking a cigarette. He was waiting on my mother to get there so he could beat on her. My daddy had a hawk knife under the chair where he was sitting in. He pulled it from under the chair and put it to her throat. He told her that he would kill her. My sisters and I started crying and screaming, and we told him to let her go. He let her go after torturing her.

Another incident I recall took place during Thanksgiving. My mother was cooking Thanksgiving dinner while everyone was sitting around and having fun. My daddy came in the house calling my mother by different obscenities and telling her that she was not worth anything. He called her the "B" word and told her that he should kill her.

He told her that she was good for nothing and knocked her on the floor. After he knocked her down, he went outside. The house that we lived in was in the woods. We had a German shepherd dog that really loved my mother. The dog would not let anyone get near her when he was around. I even considered the dog to be my guardian angel. One day my daddy jumped on my mother and broke a beer bottle over her head. It cut her very close to her temple. She managed to get away and started running through the woods. My mother appeared to be terrified. The dog took off behind her. My mother later told us that she felt blood running all over her. She eventually fell out while running.

My mother told us that the dog licked her until she came to. She got up, and the dog led her to a place where he had his puppies. There was a family that lived close by, and they took my mother to the hospital. She was so close to death and didn't even realize it. God used that dog to lead my mother to safety.

There are a lot of horror stories I could tell, but I will only tell one more. This one has to do with the time my daddy kidnapped my mother. She had left him at this point and moved into an apartment. He took her back to the house and beat her. He did some other things to her I don't care to write about. She had been missing for two days. My daddy had to leave and go out on the road.

My mother did not have any transportation so she called me to come to pick her up. It was unbelievable the way she looked. I could hardly tell that she was my mother. It was terrible.

When I was twelve years old, I made this declaration: no man will ever do to me what I have seen my father do to my mother. I always thought my father would kill my mother right in front of my eyes. I was really scared as a child. I hated to see him coming when he came in from the road. I was supposed to be daddy's little girl. He was supposed to be my first love. I was so afraid of my first love. All little girls wants their daddy to be their first love.

When this doesn't happen, there is a void placed in that child that is just waiting to be filled with whatever would take the place of that love relationship. This is why many girls find men who are no good. If the man is good, she will eventually destroy the relationship unless the relationship receives the proper intervention. If there is no intervention, she will destroy the relationship because she did not get what she needed from her father. The situation robs that child of her worthiness. It will cause that child to have very low self-esteem. They would have no clue as to who they are as a person. They will fall for anyone that would show them some attention.

I believe that to be the reason it took me a while to get married. I got married at the age of thirty-two. I really meant what I said when I was twelve years old. When I got married, I was hard core. I had this wall up that said, "If you even look like you want to do something to me, you will be a sure candidate for the hospital." There have been times when my husband would do or say something that made me think of my father, and my wall would go up. My husband has never hit me during our twenty-year marriage, but as all couples do, we have had our disagreements. My sisters know that my husband has never hit me because he is still living. I thank God that my husband is not like my father.

My husband and I were doing a study of cause and effect. We talked about things that have affected him as a result of what I had experienced. A person, who has been affected by such atrocity as I, cannot understand the effect it has on the spouse. It would take the spouse bringing these things out to give the person an idea of how he is being affected. As we shared our feelings, I was shocked by the things my husband said to me. He reminded me of how it was when we first got married. When we were entering a building, he would attempt to open the door for me, but I would open the door for myself. It got to the point where my husband would run up to the door so he could open it for me.

My husband would attempt to open the car door for me, and I would tell him that I did not need him to open the door for me. He would buy me flowers, and I would tell him not to buy me flowers because they would live only a short time, and I considered that a waste of money. I had a twelve-year-old daughter when my husband I got married. My husband attempted to discipline her, but I would not have it. I didn't realize it at the time, but I was protecting my daughter from a man who I perceived as my father. We have two daughters together, and I did the same thing with our oldest daughter. It took me a while to realize what I was doing.

My husband and I went to Florida for our nineteenth wedding anniversary. We went to St. Pete beach in St. Petersburg, Florida. My husband was paying two hundred and fifty dollars a night for an oceanfront hotel room. We were supposed to stay for a week. By the fourth day, I told him that I was ready to go back to North Carolina. I felt that he was spending too much money. When we returned home, I made that point clear to him. He made me see how I was short-changing myself. As my husband and I discussed the issues concerning cause and effect, I begin to realize why I responded the way I did. I realized that it was due to the effect my father had on me. When a child experiences a hostile childhood such as watching her father beat on her mother, it is devastating to that child.

It had such a terrible effect on me. It causes a girl to become independent. As this child grows into an adult, she has prepared herself to be independent in her marriage in case she has to fend for herself. In her mind, she is still seeing her father. If her husband mistreats her, she is prepared to live on her own. Many women remain in abusive relationships because they have nowhere to go. Some women may even end up in prostitution. They are the ones who were not prepared to take care of themselves. The relationship was so frustrating that they had to get out by any means. The ironic thing about women who have this experience is that we desire to be in a relationship.

One would think that after the experience of seeing how evil a man could be, we would not want anything to do with one. This could be the case for some of those females who are lesbians. I believe that the Bible tells us to not judge because we do not have enough sense to judge people righteously. We just do not know what experiences a person had that leads them into the lifestyle they choose. I know that there may be variances when it come to the effect of seeing a father beat up on a mother, but there are some attitudes that are conducive to all women who have this experience. Knowing this truth, I know that the principles to bring forth change are the same regardless of those variances.

Children affected by this horrible experience will need time to work through the difficulties of bringing change in their lives. It is an experience that allowed children to build up walls against men for many years. Tearing down that wall will not be an overnight experience tearing those walls down. Many years had gone by before I realized these walls had been built up. I thought I was exhibiting normal behavior. Women who have had this experience must realize how they have been affected, and how it affects to the people they are trying to relate to. Once I came to the realization that I had all of these walls up, I began praying for God to help me in tearing them down.

God spoke to me and said that He was going to help me to tear the walls down one brick at a time. While these walls were up, they had a profound effect on my relationships. During my years of no regeneration, I was involved in several relationships. I had to keep those who I was in the relationship with at arm's length. I was not going to let them get too close to me. I saw what happened to my mother, and it was not about to happen to me. I made sure that I was in control at all times. I had a job, a car, and my own place to live. I was not going to be in a position where I had to depend on a man. I was prepared to leave at any minute and did not have to be concerned with where I would go.

One of the relationships was with a man who thought he was going to beat on me. He ended up in prison. I know prison is not a good place to go, but it is better than what could have happened. I was determined that I would not be treated the way my mother was treated, and I would have defended that position by any means. My oldest sister, Shirley, told of the time she was at her doctor's office. She stated that the nurse had to ask her series of questions. One of the questions had to do with domestic violence. Her response to the question was, "I am sitting in this office, aren't I?" I suspect that all of my sisters felt the same way. We all had the same experience.

As I think back to those times, I am surprised that any of us wanted anything to do with a man. I guess nature has the stronger force.

I can't see where it had an effect on my casual relationships, or my feminine relationships. If there were any ill effects on these relationships, I would think that it had to do with the general anger I had as a result of my experience. When one is seeking to overcome the damages caused by such an experience, it is a lifelong attempt in overcoming the ramifications of such deviant experience. As I continue the process of overcoming, I'm sure I will learn even more about the adverse effects of such an experience. God still has a few more bricks to tear out of my wall.

I know one thing for certain: and that is the truth about the exasperating difficulties it causes in a marriage. I recall when my husband and I went to a day session of a convention that took place at the church we once attended. He brought some of the things that were said by my sister, who was one of the speakers that morning. He said that my sister mentioned how she had given her husband a fit. My sister had given an account of her childhood experience with our father. She alluded to the effect it had on her. My husband told me that I had given him a fit just as my sister had given her husband a fit. The effect of our experience weighed heavier in our marriage.

I believe it has to do with the greater expectations one has in a marital relationship. When a woman is dating a man or shacking up with a man, it is much easier to pick up and leave. A woman, who shares the experience I had growing up, may have emotional ties with the man she is dating, but if the pain is greater than the emotional ties, it is time to leave. The difficulty one finds in the marriage has to do with the commitment that was made in the presence of God. If the marriage is difficult, and the woman feels like there are a lot of changes to be made, she will spend a lot of time in prayer.

She will remain in the marriage with the hope that God would make or assist in the necessary adjustments that are needed. A woman who shares my experience is unaware of the difficulties she is presenting in the marriage. She thinks that there is something wrong with the husband. She is not aware that she is exhibiting abnormal responses to the situations the couple is dealing with. Our oldest daughter would come home from school and tell her daddy about someone who was bothering her in school or on the way home from school. My husband would go to the person's house and talk to the child's parent. He even confronted teachers at the school when he felt that they were being provocative.

After a period of time, I told my husband that he was crazy for doing that. Shortly after I told him that, God told me that I felt that way because I did not have a father who protected me. When God told me that, it opened up a can of worms. I then wondered what other thoughts of mine were due to the effect my father had on me. Not long after that encounter is when my husband and I started doing a study on cause and effect. I begin to realize that my experience had an effect on me not only as a wife, but as a mother also. I found myself thinking that I had to protect my children from their father. It takes a while to get that kind of experience of one's system.

When it came to my husband disciplining my children, I had to make sure that they were not harmed. I had to make sure that they did not come out damaged the way I had. I recall telling my husband that I did not want my daughter to grow up the way I did. He would tell me that growing up as I had was impossible. I had shared with him the things my sisters had to do when we were growing up. Aside from seeing our father beat up on our mother, we had to do chores that a male boy would normally do. We had to work in the garden, feed the animals, and go down to the well to retrieve water before we went to school. We did not have running water in the house.

Due to a medical problem our only brother had, he was unable to do those things. My husband would tell me that we lived in a house that had running water and that we did not have any animals or a garden. He also mentioned that she did not live in a house with a man who was beating on her mother. I had a fit when my husband gave my daughter instructions on how to clean the bathroom. I felt that he was being too meticulous with his method. He would tell me that it was not just about the bathroom, but it was also about a universal principal that facilitated catapulting into her later stages of life. I wasn't quite seeing what he was seeing.

At this point in our marriage, the only child we had was my daughter I had before we were married. After we had a child together, things were different. My husband would say that he loved my daughter as if she were his biological daughter. That had to be proved. We have two daughters that are his biological daughters. When the oldest one turned sixteen years old, I found myself hiding things she was doing from my husband because I knew he would not approve of them. She was interested in boys at that time, and I felt that my husband would be too strict on her. My husband and I went to St. Petersburg, Florida, for our wedding anniversary. God spoke to me while we were driving up along I-95.

God told me that by hiding things from my husband the way I did, it taught my daughter how to lie and scheme. That was a revelation that I was not proud of. I changed my tactics with our youngest daughter.

The terrible experience I had growing up produced some adverse ramifications. My children didn't have the experiences I had, but based on my experience and the way I felt that I had protect my children, it could have created some issues in their lives. I believe their issues pale in comparison to mine. There aren't any perfect parents, but there are parents who gave their children a better experience than what I had to endure. Although I may not have chosen the best methods, I did have good intentions.

I had to forgive myself because I could have ended up being angry all over again. I could look at the situation and blame it all on my father. I had to forgive my father. There are people who hold on to the anger and refuse to forgive. They feel as though the person owes them something, and by not forgiving them, it is causing them to pay. The truth of the matter is that the person who's holding on to the anger is the one who's paying. Holding on to the anger and not forgiving the person causes many problems for the person who's holding to the anger. It causes psychological as well as physical problems. I had to forgive my father because that same anger could have been passed on to my children.

Had I held on to the anger, I would never have realized the calling God has for my life. I had to turn my lemon into lemonade. I had to come to the realization that a loving God did not allow me to have that experience just to be mean to me. I realized that God was with me every step of the way. I would not have had the wisdom to minister to women if I did not have this experience. God calls on certain people to be leaders. There are countless women out there who are hurting and can't put their finger on the reason they are. Women would have to know why they are angry before they can start the deliverance process. That is where I come in.

CHAPTER

My Wife

I have some strange views concerning marriage. I begin this chapter's venture by talking about how I met my wife.

I was in ministerial training at the time, and part of that training was driving my pastor to his evangelistic appointments. I went to many places with my pastor and got some really good training. One such place was a church in our own town where my pastor was asked to speak. At the conclusion of my pastor's message, I saw this young lady dance from the back of the church all the way up to the front. As I sat there in amazement, I begin to hear the word marriage in my spirit. I did my best to live Holy, even to the point of turning down women who had made advances toward me.

Anyway, when I saw this woman dancing down the aisle, I heard the word *marriage* in my spirit, and the first thing I responded with was "Oh no, I'll never touch that woman." I guess I lied. Not only did I end up touching her; she bore two children from me. She was a member of the church where my pastor spoke. A few Sundays later, she was at our church. I was teaching Sunday school at the time, and she was in my Sunday school class. At some point, I began to get interested in her. There were a few things I wanted to know about her. I wanted to know if she was married and how old she was. We had a discussion one Sunday morning that prompted her to reveal that she was not married and how old she was. I didn't want to come straight out and ask her. God has His ways. She looked to be too young for me. Some people may still think she's too young. At the time, I was thirty-six, and she was thirty.

When she came to our church, she had an occasion where she sang a solo. I decided to maximize the moment. I had written several songs, and I wanted her to sing them. I made the suggestion to her, and she agreed to meet me at the church the following Monday at four o'clock. From there, we started communicating and eventually dating. We have been married twenty years, and we still haven't practiced the songs yet.

We had to go through an obstacle course to get married. I had gotten married ten years prior while I was in the military. The marriage lasted approximately four years. During that time, I was running from God instead of running to him. My pastor believed that if a person had been married before, that person could not get married again unless that person was getting married to the same person all over again. He gave me an ultimatum; he told me to stop talking to her or quit teaching Sunday school. I did not want to stop doing either one. Finally, I told him that I would stop talking to her. She and I made plans to meet in a parking lot that night.

I was in the parking lot waiting on her, and she pulled up with a smile on her face that could have won her an award. Truthfully, though, my smile probably would have won first place. She had purchased three sweaters for me. After she gave them to me, I told her what the pastor said. I informed her that we would have to stop talking. She told me to keep the sweaters. We still found a way to continue to see one another. My pastor found out, and he told me to lock myself in the church for a week and to pray and fast about the situation. It was the week of Thanksgiving. While people were at home enjoying their turkey and candied yams, I was upstairs locked up in the prophet's chamber seeking direction from God. God kept giving me the same scripture over and over. I guess I was expecting to hear God say something like

"Hey, fine as she is, you better go after that." God kept saying to me, "If you ask me for bread, will I give you a stone, and if you ask me for meat, will I give you a serpent?"

The following week, I told my pastor what God had said. He was not excited about my response. Shortly after this, my pastor told me that someone told him that my car was spotted at my wife-to-be to be house at two in the morning. This was a blatant lie. I told my pastor that it was only fair that he tell me who told him that so I could have the opportunity to confront that person. His response was that he could not tell me because more than one person said it. I kept on him until he finally told me who said it. I found out that his daughter told him that.

The following Sunday morning, I went to the church to speak with her. She would not tell me who told her that. I told her that she could have left that lie right where she found it. She started walking down the stairs crying. By the time she got to the bottom of the stairs, her father was coming into the church. She told him that I called her a liar. He told me to get out of his church and that if I ever step another foot in his church that I was going to jail. He said a lot more than that, but that was major thing that was said. A church member was standing there when he said it. She had a look on her face was indescribable. I was so hurt.

I worked at the gospel radio station at the time, and I had to go on the air that evening. I recall announcing a song before I played it. I was so messed up while I was on the air. The first name of the artist was Charles. I announced the artist as Charles Brunson. I was really torn that day. Approximately two weeks later, the pastor's daughter called me at the radio station. She told me that she realized that I did not call her a liar, but I had told her that she could have left that lie where it came from. She told me who told her. I was truly amazed. It was the daughter of the person who was standing outside of the church when I got kicked out. As time went on, it was discovered that she had lied.

My wife and I ended up joining another church by this time. Shortly after we were married, a prophet came to me and told me that God wanted me to go back to my church. It is where God wanted me to be. My wife and I went back to the church. Sometime later, my pastor told me that God told him to leave me alone because he had put that marriage together. I recall telling God that if I couldn't marry her, I did not want to marry anyone. I had it bad. My pastor was only doing what he thought was right. Many who were taught the same thing concerning marriage. The teaching came from the gospels based on what Jesus says about marriage. What a lot of people don't realize is that Jesus was only quoting the Old Testament. The new covenant of grace could not come in until after he died. Many pastors were not aware of that.

I mentioned earlier that I had some strange views on marriage. I wrote in another book, *Why "U" Do the Things "U" Do*, that I believed that God is meticulous concerning marriage. When God made a wife for Adam, He did not make several women, line them up, and then tell Adam to pick one. God made one specific woman and presented the woman to Adam. If Adam would have rejected the woman, Adam would have remained single and found a giraffe to hang out with. I believe God has remained consistent in His approach to marriage. The Bible tells us that God made them male and female. I don't believe that applies to just gender.

I believe the intended understanding of that particular scripture pertains to a specific man and a specific woman. The Bible tells us to acknowledge God in all of our ways, and He will direct our path. The Bible also states the he who finds a wife finds a good thing. If we were to follow the instructions laid out in scripture for us, we would save ourselves a lot of heartache. We are to acknowledge God concerning the mate we are to be with. He who finds a wife finds a good thing. This scripture suggests to me that a man should be the one looking. I made the mistake of not acknowledging God the first time I was married. Not only that; it was quite frivolous regarding the reason I got married.

When we take a close look at the diaspora, and a close look at the migration afterwards, we would find out that the ten northern tribes of Israel are not lost after all. We would find the descendants of these tribes in places such as Great Britain, Australia, Canada, the United States, and a few other places. When we take a close look at the Genesis account concerning creation, we will find that Adam and Eve had many children. That truth can be found in Genesis 5:4. Also, there are people who get it twisted concerning Cain and his wife. The Bible says that Cain took his wife to the land of Nod and that he knew his wife in the land of Nod. He did not find her in the land of Nod.

The Bible uses the word knew to describe a sexual encounter. The only way man could be fruitful and multiply was to know his sister. There are those who teach that there was an eighth day of creation. The teachers of that doctrine apparently did not pay any attention to what was said in Acts 7. God made the whole creation by creating one man. The people who teach the eighth-day creation also teaches that it is demonic to speak in tongues. In the book of Acts when the disciples decided that they did not have the time to wait on table, that they needed to choose seven men, and that they had to be full of the Holy Spirit to be qualified to do so, they set forth the qualification for ministry.

When one is full of the Holy Spirit, one will speak in tongues. It is very clear then, the people who teach against speaking in tongues are not qualified to do ministry. If one were to look at the big picture, it would be clear that from somewhere down the line, a man married his sister. I believe that there is one specific man for a woman and vice versa.

An interesting thing happened to me on Friday, March 9, 2012, at 9 a.m. God told me two things: He told me that the angels were preparing the white horse for Jesus's return and that I was a descendent from the tribe of Issachar. God lead me to my wife who could possibly be a descendent from the same tribe. God knows who is best for whom. God put two people together who had serious issues. Based on the issues my wife had to overcome, I consider her to be quite credible. I think it would be fitting to also mention her authority. As children of the kingdom, we all have authority. I have a philosophy concerning that matter that may differ from others philosophy. I believe that according to the way we suffer, after we overcome the suffering, we are then qualified to facilitate the ability for others to overcome.

Consider 2 Corinthians 1–7: "Blessed be the God and Father of our Lord Jesus Christ, the Father of mercies and God of all comfort, who comforts us in all of our tribulation, that we may be able to comfort those who are in any trouble, with the comfort with which we ourselves are comforted by God. For as the sufferings of Christ abound in us, so our consolation also abounds through Christ. Now if we are afflicted, it is for your consolation and salvation, which is effective for enduring the same sufferings, which we also suffer. If we are comforted, it is for your consolation and salvation. Our hope for you is steadfast, because we know that as you are partakers of the sufferings, so also you will partake in the consolation."

I don't think the scripture need any elaboration on it. I spoke to another pastor at one point and told him the same thing I mentioned as my philosophy, and he was in total opposition of it. The word speaks for itself. When I review the things my wife suffered, I can plainly see the authority she has to minister to others who've had the same of similar sufferings. Authority in this case equates to an anointing of divine enablement. She is able to break the bond of afflictions in the lives of those God has called her to minister to. She has such an awesome ministry. There are so many abused women in and outside of the church community.

As the husband of such anointed woman, I have to be very careful as to not take her anointing for granted. I can't just see her as my wife. She is more than the beautiful and sexy woman I married. She's my wife, she's my girlfriend, she's my children's mother, but more than that, she's God's anointed servant. I must always be mindful of that. It is necessary for me to think of that so it would allow me to pardon all of her shortcomings and see her for the real person that she is. My wife is frequently called on to speak at someone's church.

By word of mouth, people who hear her at one church, will go back and tell others about her. People experience the anointing on her, and then see the necessity to call on her for ministry. I have to say a few things concerning her knowledge. My wife grew up having to work in the garden prior to her going to school each morning. She completed high school but was not interested in furthering her education. I found out there is nothing like having a good ol' country girl. She told me that she and sisters had had to feed the animals, work the garden, and go down to the well to get water—all before going to school each morning. She had a brother, but he was unable to assist them due to a medical problem.

That may have had something to do with her not wanting to further her education. As soon as she was old enough to do so, she wanted to be on her own. Although she had not obtained the level of education I had reached, she had knowledge that went far beyond the classroom. She told me that she spent a lot of time in church as a child. On Sundays, it was an all-day thing. She stated that she really liked going to church. To this very day, she is always checking around to see who's having some type of church service. A lot of people like going to ball games, festivals, nightclubs, and the like. But not her. Give her a church service, and she is in paradise.

Her knowledge was obtained through the school of life. She took Hard Knocks 101. She took what life taught her and coupled it with what God's word taught her, and she is a piece of knowledge going somewhere to give it away. During my later years of studying the effects of childhood on adulthood, my wife gave me some information that set me on a new path. She would get revelations from God while we are traveling. We were on our way back from a visit in Norfolk, Virginia, and all of a sudden, she gave the answer I had been searching for. There were other times she got revelations while we were traveling.

I'll get the answers to all of my questions. Someone is always calling her on the phone to get some type of direction for his or her situation. There were times she was on the phone, and I was thinking, "Hey, what about me?" I always gave her the space she needed. She knows how to put everything aside and say, "Okay, your turn." As the third of seven girls, she was the first one to enter into the kingdom. The rest of the sisters followed her footsteps. At the age of fifty-two, she is now going back to school. She is attending a college in our area and is studying early childhood education. I believe it will assist her in understanding herself and those she was called to minister to.

I will say a little concerning her wisdom. Wisdom is different from knowledge. It is one thing to have knowledge and understanding, but wisdom takes on a whole new meaning. It is good to have knowledge and understanding, but without the wisdom to apply it, it is like not having knowledge and understanding at all.

I recall many years ago when I was speaking to one of my brothers about which college to attend. He told me that he wanted to go to Howard University because, according to his research, he had learned it was valuable. He told me that the majority of the instructors in the field he was going into, which was business, had their own businesses. My brother said that he wanted to learn from people who had knowledge outside of the classroom. He felt that he would better informed by those who were actually doing what they were teaching. He went to Howard University and received his degree in business administration. Many years have gone by since then, and I have found his conclusion to be correct. As I stated earlier, my wife didn't learn what she knows in a classroom, she has firsthand experience concerning the ministry God has chosen her for. She is a woman of wisdom. She is my special gift from God.

It is very important for me to recognize who she is. If I fail to recognize the true person inside, I could cause myself a lot of pain. The Bible tells us to know no man by the flesh. We must know the spirit of the person. The spirit is the real person. There is a lot that I can say about that, but I do not want to go off on a tangent. My wife goal's in life is to teach other women to be overcomers.

I know that I have some weird ideas when it comes to the plans of God. I have an idea that I'd like to present here. Some may consider it as being in left field, while others may agree with it. It begins with the sovereignty of God. We know that God is omniscience. With that being true, we must realize that God is aware of what we will go through in life.

If we nostalgically look over the rotten things in our lives, we must ask the question, "Why? Why would a loving God who loved us so much as to give His only son as a ransom for all, then turn around and allow such pain, grief, heartache, and other emotional maladies in our lives?" It doesn't seem to make sense, and it could never make any sense to the carnal mind. A spiritual-minded person might find a silver lining in that dark cloud. I think we are looking at a paradox here. There are those who would find this as being controversial, but I see it as a paradox.

The carnal mind would probably go as far as to say that God is showing Himself of being a bit bipolar. It's as if God was having such a good day and decided to do the most benevolent thing that could be done in the entire universe, and just a few days later decided that he could not stand his creation. It's as if he remembered the Genesis account concerning fall of man and said to himself, "I'm going to get those hardheaded misfits." That would be quite tragic. It is my opinion that we do not have that kind of God, so it leads me to a theological argument. I believe in the purpose and design of God. I believe that those tragic events in our lives are designed as a preparation for our purpose.

I take you back to the title of this book: Are your children out of control? Remember that the children I'm speaking of are your inner children. A woman who's seen her mother get beaten daily would grow up with many walls against men. As a result, the husband who marries this female has a task of a serious burden barer. He is in a relationship with a woman who can barely stand him. I'm sure many men have walked out of these relationships because of the pressure he finds himself under. It is a very difficult situation to deal with. The Bible tells the man to dwell with her according to knowledge. The problem many men have in such relationships is ignorance.

Some men leave these relationships shaking their head. The relationship has been over for ten or more years and he's still trying to figure her out. That woman is forty-five years old but her inner child is four years old. All she can see in her husband is her father. It would take a man of understanding to stay in that relationship to help her work through it. In the mean time, he has to deal with his own issues.

I believe that God pairs us up in such a way as to allow us to work our issues out simultaneously. It is like the male and female ends of an electrical wire. If two male ends get together, the results could be tragic. The male–female end is a metaphor for the complimentary issues.

Although both mates have these weaknesses, both mates have certain strengths. The man's strengths have to compliment the woman's weaknesses. God knows how to put people together. He is just awesome like that. That is why the Bible says that He made them male and female, and that does not just pertain to gender. My mind wants to go in three or four different ways, but I'm going to concentrate on one area so I can make this short and sweet.

If there is a group of people in a room, let's say there are four adults and a twelve-year-old. If a seven-year-old girl enters the room, she is going to relate to the twelve-year-old. She will attempt to relate to the person closest to her age. The same is true when it comes to forty-five-year-old women whose inner child is four years old. When there is a dispute between a father and his nineteen-year-old daughter, the inner child in that forty-five-year-old will relate to that nineteen-year-old.

The husband feels rejected and disrespected because he is aware of what the Bible says concerning the order of merit: God, Jesus, husband, children. That is the order for the wife. The order for the husband goes like this: God, Jesus, wife, children. A wife or husband are not supposed to put children before their mate. Any time God's order is reversed, the results are tragic.

These hardships are what my wife had to overcome and what she must teach other women to overcome. God always has leaders. The Bible tells the older women to teach the younger women. When the teaching is absent, the result is a Christian marriage gone down the drain. The inner children never grew up. It would be tragic for a forty-year-old man to marry a twelve-year-old girl and expect the marriage to work. So many men are not aware of the root cause of their problems. If the man doesn't settle his issues, which are presented to him by the woman with her issues, and vice versa, the result could be devastating. God is not bipolar; He knows exactly what He is doing. We must get the revelation on His way of doing things.

I would like to briefly summarize my wife's abilities. I recall some years ago when she would tell me that she was a strong black woman. She was in her assessment. I would go as far as to say that she was bit too strong. A lot of her strength came from a statement she told me she made at the age of twelve. She told me that that she told herself that no man would ever do to her what she saw her father do to her mother as he beat her. I know from experience that she meant that. She had me scratching my head during those early years of our marriage.

That is where the three stages of my marriage come in. The first stage was the weird woman stage. I could not understand why my wife would not let me open the door for her. It got to the point that I would hurry to get to a door when we entered a building so I could open her door. She did not want me to open the door for her. She told me that she could open her own door. I tried buying her flowers. She told me that she did not like flowers. She said that eventually they would just die. I would tell her that she was the finest woman in the world. She would tell me that she didn't need to hear that. I would say, "This woman is weird." I call that the weird woman stage.

Approximately twelve years had passed by, and by that time God started revealing to me what it was I was experiencing. I would then tell myself that I was paying for what her father did to her. So that was the unfair payment stage. Several years of telling myself that ended with the realization that I had a job to do. That would be called the understanding stage.

The four stages of a marriage start with the ecstasy stage. This is the stage when she could do no wrong. The next stage is the conscious stage. I began to realize her faults. The next stage is the conflict stage. This is the stage when we go home to visit mom, and mom would begin to get suspicious. Mom was feeling a bit lonely during that ecstasy stage because the husband wants to spend all his time with his wife. During the conflict stage, mom begins to get a little tired of her son. The final stage is the resolution stage. Statistics say that a little over 50 percent of marriages do not reach this stage. Those in marriages that reach this stage are couples who have worked through the issues or just decided to accept each other weaknesses. The thing that got me excited is when my wife realized the effects of her father on her life. It is through her understanding of this that gave her the motivation to start working on the matter. Now she is able to help other women who had this same experience. Three days prior to me writing this, my wife went to speak at a woman's conference. She told me of an instance when she had to personally minister to some women who were full of pain. She also stated that if people in the church would be honest, we would find countless of women who are hurting. My wife has the ability to help them.

CHAPTER

One Plus One Equals One

God's mathematical system is much different from our human system. The Bible tells us that one can put a thousand to flight, and two can put ten thousand to flight. It would seem that by man's standards that two would be able to put two thousand to flight. According to the human mathematical system, one plus one equals two. God said that the two should become one flesh. Marriage is the most oxymoronic institution on the planet. We get married for the pleasure of companionship, and we find ourselves experiencing lots of pain. We look for love, and we find ourselves fighting hatred. We expect peace, and we find ourselves experiencing World War III.

Well, I do not consider myself a relationship expert, but after twenty years of marriage, I do have something to say. A lot of our marital issues stem from the inner children being out of control. I recall back when I was studying developmental psychology the subject came up concerning children who grew up without a father. I gave my input on the matter and received a response from two women who had that experience.

One young woman had recently finished high school. Her response was that she didn't see where she was experiencing any maladies as a result of not having a father active in her life. I asked her if she was married, and she said no. I told her to keep living. The second was an older woman who gave the same response. She also indicated that she was not where she wanted to be in life. I asked her if she was sure that by her not having a father active in her life had anything to do with her current position. She thought about it and decided that it could have had an effect on her current position. A father's role is to provide, protect, teach, and nurture his children. It is God's divine design to have a father in the house. When God's design is perverted, the results can be devastating. A father sets the example of how the woman is supposed to be treated by a man. An absent, inactive, or abusive father presents grave issues in the life of his children.

Many of these issues do not show up until the person is married. It is in the marital relationship where the inner children find opportunities to express themselves. The becoming one in a marriage is a matter of training those inner children to become responsible adults. It takes a godly foundation to stand on before the principles for change can be applied. The first entry into change is to admit that the issues exist. People go many years living in denial. The mask is worn to prevent those on the outside from knowing the real person. The people who are wearing the mask do not like what's under the mask. The realization of one not liking himself or herself is a sure way to know others wouldn't either.

In a discussion such as this one, culture and community must be mentioned. A culture will influence a community. A good definition of culture is this: the sum total of the attainments and learned behavior patterns of any specific period, race, or people. A community can be defined as thus: a group of people living together or in one locality and subject to the same laws, having common interest, and so on. Many different communities make up a country, and they can destroy the country. Within the communities are families. The families can destroy the communities. The strength of the community comes from the strength of the families. The strength of a family is determined by how that family was cultivated.

When we break down the culture to the family level, we find the place from where our attitudes stem. We will find certain habits that were obtained from the family culture. We take those same habits into our relationships. Although the family's laws should be based on the laws of the community, there is some latitude with the ways these laws are carried out.

For instance, I grew up where the house had to be cleaned up every Saturday. Another person grew up in a house where as the house had to be cleaned every Friday. It is a good thing to keep a clean house. It could make the difference in being healthy or sick. It is not wrong to clean up Saturdays any more than it is wrong to clean up Fridays.

However, it could pose a problem for a couple in which the husband cleans up on Saturdays and the wife cleans up Fridays. The wife could be overly adamant concerning the house being cleaned up on Fridays. It could be such a problem that it leads to other problems. The way I would deal with a situation like that is weigh the situation on the scale of scripture. If there were no Biblical law governing the matter, then I would submit to my wife. In those instances where there is no Biblical law present, a man would do good to let his wife have her way. It makes things go a lot easier in the bedroom. That is the easy solution to becoming one. The difficult part has to do with those issues we brought into the marriage from childhood.

These are issues that will not allow us to respond in a mature manner. If a person has been rejected all of his or her life, that person will find it very difficult to respond to rejection in the marriage. It takes outside intervention to bring out the root of the problem and to offer the principles that would bring forth change. To become one flesh is to do whatever is necessary to overcome those issues that facilitate our efforts to become one flesh. Some people refer to the flesh as only the body. The flesh is also conducive to one's thinking. To bring a husband's and wife's thinking together takes nothing less than a miracle.

I have heard men say in times past that women were crazy. I have also heard women say the same thing about men. It's just a matter of our thinking being opposite. There is no negative without a positive. There is no left without a right. There is no back without a front, and there is no up without a down. It takes two opposites coming together as one to make life the way God intended it to be. God tells the husband to love his wife the way Christ loves the church. That is not a suggestion; it is a commandment. Men who had an absent, inactive, or abusive fathers will run into difficulties when attempting to apply this principle. Those inner children like to show up in the middle of this attempt. They are like roaches that only show up when company is over. They will have themselves a ball.

Twenty years ago during the first year of my marriage, I attempted to love my wife as Christ loved the church. I found out that I really didn't know what that meant. I decided that I was going to find out. I needed desperately to understand my wife. I was in the weird woman stage at this time. I went out and brought several cases of Gatorade and water, and I told God that I would not let a piece of solid food touch my lips until I got the answer that I needed. The day I set out to start my fast, the Lord spoke to me as if He and I were looking at each other face to face. God gave me an answer to a question that I had concerning my wife. I asked God some questions concerning loving my wife.

I told God that the scripture was too broad and that I needed a meticulous explanation of what it meant to love my wife as Christ loves the church. I told God that I could not die for her the way Jesus died for me. At the time this took place, I had been in a terrible car accident. I was going through an intersection when someone driving a truck missed the stop sign, and he crashed right into me. He must have been driving really fast because he totaled my car. I was so injured that I was out of work for an entire year. I was going back and forth to the doctor at that time.

Because my car had been totaled, when I was able to drive again, I had to always wait until my wife got back with the car. It was so inconvenient for me.

God used that situation to explain to me what the scripture meant. God told me that if my wife wanted to go somewhere with the car, I was to allow her to do so. My response to God was this: "You mean I am supposed to sit in this house with nothing to do but be miserable?" God told me that by planting into her in this manner, my wife would in turn be a blessing to me by being very considerate. That statement put me on the course to also understanding what sow and reap meant. God further told me that the only time I could have the car when she wanted it was when He was sending me out to minister.

God shared other things with me, but that was the thing that stuck out the most. I had bought all of that Gatorade and water, and God spoke to me on the first day. God knew I was serious about what I said. If I ended up looking like a pole, I would have been a pole with a word from the Lord. A man loving his wife the way Christ loves the church takes a man outside of himself, but this verse does the same for the women: "Wives, submit to your husband." Here is where I get in trouble. I have been in environments where women had a real problem with this scripture. I have a theory on why women are reluctant to following this scripture.

I can remember when a cigarette came out that was specifically for women; the commercial for it had a woman saying, "We've come a long way, baby." Women were treated as second-class citizens. There was a time when women could not vote in America. When I was a boy, I saw very few married women driving cars. My father would take my mother where she wanted to go. I saw a lot of families doing the same thing. I can only remember two women who drove. I never knew my mother to work outside of the house. There were eight children, and my father took care of our family's welfare by himself. There were three boys and five girls. My father did not believe in his boys washing dishes. I must say that I was not mad at him at all. The boys took care of the outside of the house.

I can also remember people saying that girls were made of sugar, spice, and everything nice and that boys were made of frogs, nails, and puppy dog tails. What a comparison. I believe that according to the pressure that was placed on woman as second-class citizens, women are very careful not to fall back into that mode again. It had to be a really hard situation that women came out of because they are reluctant to obeying God's instructions on submission. I also believe that men don't understand what submission is. I think we tend to go overboard with that scripture. We have the propensity to forget about the scripture that tells us to submit one to another.

To get the real meaning of submission, both verses of loving the wife and submitting to the husband need to be studied. A wife not being able to submit to her husband puts a lot of pressure on the relationship where the four stages of marriage are concerned. During the first stage of marriage, which is the ecstasy stage, the husband can't see any wrong in the woman. She can get away with murder during this stage. This stage differs in terms of longevity from couple to couple. It may be a short time for some couples. It may take a few years for other couples. Whatever the case, it doesn't last forever. Some marriages have to function off commitment for a while. The ecstasy stage is the stage with few arguments. The next stage, which is the conscious stage, can bring on many arguments. Couples will begin to question themselves on why they bothered getting married. The man becomes aware of every fault the woman has. If the man is unaware of how to choose his battles, he may find himself in love's junkyard. The conscious stage takes the couple into the conflict stage. That is where the sparks start flying. Every flaw is well-known at this point. These flaws can either make or break the marriage. Statistics says that fifty percent of the marriages do not make it past this stage. It is believed that the percentage is slightly elevated in the church community. I'm sure the reason for that is due to the enemy targeting God-ordained marriages. If a marriage is not glorifying God, the enemy is happy with it.

I decided that my wife was perfect. After going through the conflict stage of marriage, there is a decision to make. One must sit down and weigh the two sides. On one side is the list of what I so appreciate about her. On the other side is the list of what can be improved on. That side is much shorter than the other side. I'm reminded of the eighty-twenty rule right now. If the eighty is on the appreciative side, I consider the woman perfect. That's as perfect as it is going to get. That philosophy puts me in the resolve stage.

I suspect she is in the resolve stage. She does everything she can to see that I'm happy. She gives me food, she gives me water, and she gives me love. Many people are experiencing difficulties in their relationships, and can't seem to come together on things. My hopes is that after reading this book, the reader is enlightened to the point that whatever difficulties are being experienced, whether it has to do with a relationship or otherwise, he or she can overcome the hardships. The reader is now able to understand the root cause of those issues and begin to apply the principles to get those children under control.